# Chevrolet History:
# 1958-1960

## By John D. Robertson

Library of Congress Cataloging-In-Publication Date ISBN 1-880524-44-9

Published by **Cars & Parts Magazine,**
The Voice of the Collector Car Hobby Since 1957

Cars & Parts Magazine is a division of Amos Press Inc.,
911 Vandemark Road, Sidney, Ohio 45365

**Also publishers of:**

Catalog of American Car ID Numbers 1950-59
Catalog of American Car ID Numbers 1960-69
Catalog of American Car ID Numbers 1970-79
Catalog of Camaro ID Numbers 1967-93
Catalog of Chevy Truck ID Numbers 1946-72
Catalog of Ford Truck ID Numbers 1946-72
Catalog of Chevelle, Malibu & El Camino ID Numbers 1964-87
Catalog of Pontiac GTO ID Numbers 1964-74
Catalog of Corvette ID Numbers 1953-93
Catalog of Mustang ID Numbers 19641/2-93
Catalog of Thunderbird ID Numbers 1955-93
Catalog of Firebird ID Numbers 1967-93
Catalog of Oldsmobile 4-4-2, W-Machine &
   Hurst/Olds ID Numbers 1964-91
Catalog of Chevy Engine V-8 Casting Numbers 1955-93
Ultimate Collector Car Price Guide
Ultimate Muscle Car Price Guide
Automobiles of America
Salvage Yard Treasures of America
Corvette: American Legend (The Beginning)
Corvette: American Legend (1954-55 Production)
Corvette: American Legend (1956-Racing Success)

Corvette: American Legend (1957-Fuel Injection/283 V-8)
Corvette: American Legend (1958-60)
Pictorial History of Chevrolet, 1929-39
Pictorial History of Chevrolet, 1940-54
Pictorial History of Chevrolet, 1955-57
Ford Country, Volume 1
Ford Country, Volume 2
Bowties of the Fifties
The Resurrection of Vicky
Peggy Sue – 1957 Chevrolet Restoration
Suzy Q.: Restoring a '63 Corvette Sting Ray

# Dedication

This is my fourth book and, most likely, my last. My pal, soulmate and wife, Catherine, has helped keep me focused. She has helped me keep the piles of research material under control when it threatened to take over room after room. She has brought me countless glasses of cold diet cola and ice water as I've sat at the computer or pushed the lawn mower around the yard. When I rub out a car she always says it looks better. She has helped me in the transition to retirement and tolerated all my get-rich-quick schemes, each of which has cost more than I could afford. (Watch out for high-tech stocks on Nasdac, they may not be what they seem to be.) She gets excited about pole barns, thinks a Thunderbird would be fun and has great taste in almost everything.

Since 1964 I have attended almost every AACA Fall Meet at Hershey. Magnificent. Almost unbelievable. I would like to thank all the people who have worked so hard behind the scenes to put those meets together every year. Hey guys! We really do notice and we really do appreciate it. Thanks.

Some years ago, maybe in the late '70s, I met a guy at Chevrolet Product Information who had old car staff all over his walls. Lou Ironside is still at GM and still a car guy and, incidentally, a craftsman in many disciplines. Lou has several beautiful woodie wagons, a couple of early '30s Fords, a muscle car Skylark, a nice early Mustang, a beautiful '40 Buick convertible resto-rod and is now building a '36 Cord rod. Lou and I have been traveling to the swap meets, near and far, for some years now and he is always good company. He has worked on many of my "projects", even the Chrysler products. He doesn't make jokes about my Studebakers. He has cheerfully dragged lots of my mistakes around on his '69 GMC car hauler. What a guy.

# Contents

# Preface

This is the fourth, and last, book in the Chevrolet Pictorial History series. Although I have several 1960s and 1970s cars in my collection, the cars I really love are those of the late '20s through the early '60s. Because these books are a labor of love, and because I can't get very excited about newer cars, I think the time has come to hang it up and spend my time on other old car pursuits. I am very happy that I've had the opportunity to share these wonderful old photos with you and, at risk of boring those who have seen the three previous prefaces, I'll give you a brief history of how this came about. Like most large companies, General Motors photographically documented the development, production and marketing efforts of its products. Some of General Motors' divisions are over 100 years old and there are images in the GM Media Archives, which are at least that old. The nucleus of the archives is the collection of the former GM Photographic. In the mid 1950s that collection was moved to a large, dingy room on the 9th floor of the Argonaut B building on Milwaukee Avenue behind Detroit's General Motors building. This room was filled with rows of floor to ceiling file drawers. Over the years, during good financial years and tough years as well, the files grew and received occasional maintenance. The photo files weren't really a secret but they weren't very accessible either. There were rumors about the treasure trove on the 9th floor and once in a while a journalist would manage to get in for a look. Some years ago Terry Boyce, former editor of *Old Cars Weekly* and the author of several Chevrolet books, was allowed in and turned loose to conduct research. A few years later, another enthusiast, whose identity is unknown to me, was given unescorted access to the collection. As it turned out, this individual tried to go home with a small mountain of images. To the best of my knowledge, that was the last time a visitor was allowed unescorted access.

In the late 1980s someone figured out that there was a gold mine on the 9th floor and an initiative was begun to collect, in one place, all such collections within GM. A system was established to electronically scan and store significant images for future retrieval and duplication. The original negatives are being preserved in a new, more environmentally friendly facility where deterioration will be less of a threat to their long-term survival. As this is being written, the identification process is nearing completion. The now 80-year-old General Motors building was donated to the State of Michigan and the archives is preparing to leave the Argonaut building for a new home in the Detroit area.

In the fall of 1999 I packed up my papers, model cars and boom box and went home for the last time. I enjoyed my six years in Argonaut B and hope that you enjoy this little slice of the history it housed.

# About the Author

**John Robertson**

**J**ohn Robertson is a retired General Motors employee who, as this is written, is keeping busy working as a part-time contract employee in Detroit area automotive archives. John was born into an automotive family on April 7, 1937. John's maternal grandfather was employed at Dodge Brothers painting Ford components at the time of his death in 1913, leaving two babies and an expecting wife. Shortly after John's mother was born, his grandmother joined Ford Motor Co. winding Model T coils at the Highland Park plant. About that time, his father's uncle left Pittsburgh to join Packard as a tool and die maker. In 1927 his father migrated to Detroit to attend night school at The Detroit College of Law. By day he operated a press at Dodge Main in Hamtramck. Arriving at work one day he was greeted by banners proclaiming that Dodge was now a product of Chrysler Corporation. Transferring to Chrysler Engineering as a lobby boy he eventually earned his law degree and spent his career in personnel. Having a relative "on the inside," many of John's relatives became Chrysler employees. Some of them moved on to other companies. Ford, General Motors, Hudson and Kaiser-Frazer all employed relatives over the years.

John, being a lifelong car guy, has worked for the car companies or their advertising and merchandising agencies for about 40 of the last 45 years. Directly or indirectly, he has served Chrysler, General Motors, Ford and Toyota. He also tried teaching school and selling cars. He has four grown daughters, Jeanne, Jill, Lynne and Julie. All are married and live in Michigan. He has three granddaughters, and two grandsons. He also has two step-grandchildren. He thinks they are all wonderful.

John's first car, a 1929 Model A Tudor, was an eighth grade graduation present. By the time he graduated from Redford High School in 1955, he had a good-sized fleet of '30s and '40s cars scattered around the neighborhood. Forty-five years later John is still looking for places to stash a few cars but promises to cutback from 20 to about 10 very soon.

John and Catherine are soul mates. They were married in 1998. Catherine, as it turns out, is a car lover with about as much self control as John. Catherine's portion of the fleet consists of a nice original 1977 Corvette, a Chevy-powered but stock-appearing 1948 Plymouth coupe, and a neat mild custom 1996 GMC Vandura that is now being used to move furniture to the winter place in DeLand, Florida. John and Catherine are looking forward to doing some winter cruising in their Chevy-powered 1948 Chrysler sedan and their 1970 Impala convertible. Next spring the snowbirds will return to Shelby Township, Mich. and again prepare to enjoy, in addition to Catherine's fleet, a 1937 De Soto convertible sedan, 1947 and 1958 Cadillac limousines, 1962 Studebaker Lark Daytona, 1959 Dodge Sierra Custom Spectator wagon, Chevy-powered 1948 Ford Fordor and a 1942 Packard.

# Introduction

The year 1958 was the sixth year of the Eisenhower administration. The United States was at peace and Ike was a popular father figure. He would soon be dealing with a rotund bully named Nikita Krushchev who replaced Nikolai Bulganin as Chairman of the Soviet Council of Ministers. Gasoline was still cheap, averaging less than 31 cents a gallon. The United Arab Republic was proclaimed with Syria, the Sudan and Egypt joining together under the leadership of the President of Egypt (this would ultimately affect those 31-cent gallons of gas). Technology was moving right along with the arrival of the Boeing 707. It cost four cents to mail a first class letter and the Brooklyn Dodgers moved to Los Angeles. The Chipmunks burst on the music scene and Bobby Darin recorded a sentimental little number called "Splish Splash" while the more mature folks seemed to prefer Duke Ellington's "Satin Doll."

The American auto industry had been riding high in the early part of 1957 but sales flattened in the summer and finally fell. When the 1958 models were announced there were fewer buyers then there bad been when the 1957 models arrived. The situation continued to deteriorate into a full-blown recession. During 1958 one third of the nation's major industrial centers had substantial unemployment rates. In fact, unemployment reached 5.1 million, a new postwar high. Obviously, the nation's automakers were going to work harder to sell fewer cars. To make matters worse, the public did not like some of those new 1958 cars as well as they had their predecessors. That was true of both face lifted and totally restyled vehicles. Ford, a style leader in 1957, adopted a package of unrelated styling cues that seemed to be in conflict with one another. The quad taillights and sculptured decklid lacked the bold good looks of the 1957 with its pair of large round taillights bracketing a large flat decklid. The quad headlights were almost mandatory if you wanted to sell cars in 1958 but, when combined with the massive bumper-grille ensemble and the new hood blister that flowed back from a rather delicate simulated air scoop, the resulting guppy face lacked the forward thrusting flair of the 1957 Fords. Some of the all-new designs missed the mark as well. Buick, which had a clean and contemporary line of cars in 1957, went for bulk in 1958. Then Buick chromed and re-chromed it. Oldsmobile and Cadillac traveled the same road to excess. No, make that extreme excess. Chrysler Corporation made minor changes to the all-new for 1957 models. Probably the worst thing it did was get rid of those wonderful 1957 Plymouth cone shaped wheel covers. Studebaker, not really a factor by now, added a pair of tack-on fins and a pair of bulbous pods to achieve the strangest quad headlight arrangement yet.

The 1958 Chevrolet was a dramatic design which effectively avoided the excesses and errors of proportion which made the senior GM cars so laughable. The youthful buyers very warmly received the new Impala models in the Bel Air series while the traditional Chevrolet buyer was completely comfortable with the other Bel Air models. Young America had been gravitating to Chevrolet since the introduction of the 265 V-8 in 1955, mostly on the basis of mechanical excellence. Now, they were being captivated by Chevrolet's styling excellence. The new 348 V-8 was almost overkill.

The poor health of the economy rained on Chevrolet's parade in 1958. While handily outselling Ford, Chevrolet was competing for fewer buyers in a recession year and didn't really reach the sales numbers that the product deserved. There were fewer qualified buyers and the mood of some of those qualified buyers was getting ugly. For a variety of reasons, including quality control disappointments, a growing number of buyers were leaning to fuel efficient, smaller imported vehicles. This return to functional simplicity was noted early by American Motors, which simultaneously discontinued the large Nash and Hudson models and re-introduced the 100-inch wheelbase Rambler, now called the American.

As 1959 rolled around Cuba acquired a new Premier, Fidel Castro. The importation of American cars and replacement parts ceased soon thereafter. The Cuban public continues patching a fleet of wheezing pre-1960 American cars. Alaska became the 49th state and Hawaii became the 50th state in 1959. In July, Vice-President Nixon traveled to Moscow where he and Nikita Krushchev engaged in the famed "kitchen debate." In another fight, Sweden's Ingemar Johansson knocked out Floyd Patterson to become the world's heavyweight champion. On February 2, Buddy Holly, a young Texan whose music had great youth-appeal, died in a plane crash along with The Big Bopper and Ritchie Vallens, creating legends that are still popular cruise night topics.

The economic pinch eased a bit in 1959 and many of the folks who had bought 1955-1957 (keep in mind that cars were usually paid off in two-to-three years at that time) vehicles were ready for a new ride.

Chevrolet, riding the crest of public approval for the 1958 Impala, was ready for another home run with the radical, all-new 1959 models. Ford had new sheet metal too. Ford was betting that the public, stung by the poor quality of many 1955-1957 models and sobered by an ugly recession, would respond to the sincerity of a squared-off conservative design. Plymouth added new front and rear ends to the 1957-1958 product and concentrated on trying to fix the many flaws of those predecessors.

The 1959 Chevrolet was one of those cars that couldn't be ignored. You had to love it or hate it. It looked huge because it was huge. A long, low beauty with dramatic lines everywhere you looked. The Ford, on the other hand, while certainly not dumpy, was not going to offend anyone. It was an acceptable compromise for the family in which one spouse loved the Chevrolet and the other hated it. The 1959 Ford, with a return to the traditional round taillights, was probably viewed by most Americans as a definite improvement over the 1958 model. Ford promoted the squared off profile as being Thunderbird inspired. The December arrival of the Galaxie model with a very formal roofline seemed to validate the Thunderbird relationship. In 1959, Ford would regain much of' the ground that was lost to Chevrolet in 1958, coming close enough to make it a cliffhanger.

Studebaker, nearly moribund in 1958, chopped the front and rear overhang off its old sedans, added a pair of wagons, a hardtop, and a cute convertible. The Lark, as it was called, was an instant, if temporary success and joined the Rambler as home-grown alternatives to the European imports that were becoming the symbol of consumer discontent with ever larger cars. In Asia, the tiny Japanese auto industry turned out 79,000 passenger cars. To put this in perspective, consider that Chevrolet turned out 72,765 Impala convertibles that model year.

The year 1960 is, perhaps, best remembered for the tenseness of cold war confrontations and angry proclamations from leaders of The Soviet Union, Cuba and the free world. On May 1, American U2 pilot, CIA agent, Francis Gary Powers was shot down by Russian ground-to-air missiles. In November, Americans elected John F. Kennedy President of the United States by an extremely narrow margin of the popular vote. Americans were listening to Roy Orbison's *Only the Lonely* and dancing to Chubby Checker's *The Twist*. They also went to the theatre to be scared to death by Hitchcock's *Psycho* or entertained by *The Apartment*. There was one passenger car registered for every three Americans.

It was an unfortunate fact of life in those years that a high-volume manufacturer better not get too far ahead of the pack or it would surely lose the conservative buyer. Chevrolet watched the conservative Fords flying out of showrooms in 1959. This year, Chevrolet received a facelift designed to make the car look less radical. The distinctive "cat-eyes" taillights were replaced by a series of small round lights in a full-width cove and the smooth sweep of the "gull wings" was flattened. Viewed from the front, the "nostrils" and the multi-piece grille were gone in favor of an inoffensive, almost generic look. (Can you tell that the author really liked that 1959 design?).

In 1960 it was Ford's turn to wow the pubic with a touch of the radical styling (yeah, the author thought that one was pretty neat, too). In profile, the front fenders and hood took on a distinct slope. The new fluid look worked best with the convertible, two-door hardtop and station wagons. The more angular roofline of four-door models and post two-doors was not as comfortable with the sleek lower body. Again, the public was slow to take to a new design and sales of the new full-size Ford were well below those of the rather conservative 1959 model. So much for innovation.

Every so often, in spite of all the checks and balances in the approval process for a new car, some truly amazing example of bizarre styling will appear and everybody not connected with the thing will ask, "What were they thinking?" The 1960 Plymouth, while rather tame compared to the 2001 Aztec, was one of those. Fortunately for Chrysler, the 1960 Dodge Dart, sharing the Plymouth's Unibody shell, was a nice looking car at about the same price, so the only losses were borne by Plymouth dealers who now had the compact Valiant to keep them afloat. The Valiant was fairly radical in its own right (the author confesses a fondness for this one too), but buyers of cars in a new segment tend to be innovators.

Chevrolet's new Corvair was done with a clean sheet of paper, utilizing some concepts near and dear to Volkswagen. The air-cooled horizontally opposed rear engine layout had been winning friends for its ability to travel in snow and sand. The author guesses that a fair number of Corvairs were sold on the basis of the VW's sterling reputation and the perception that the Corvair was just a larger VW with fresh styling. At the other end of the spectrum, the Ford Falcon was very familiar to Americans. It looked like the generic car scaled down to compact dimensions. It was even powered by a generic looking L-6.

American Motors and Studebaker continued to congratulate themselves on their good taste and good sense and the public agreed in large enough numbers to keep them in the game. It was in 1960 that the first Nissan was sold in the United States. It was the Europeans though, VW, Renault, Fiat, Morris, Hillman, Peugeot, Simca, English Ford and a few others, who were having their way with disillusioned American car buyers as the decade of the '60s was rolled out. Read on.

The new Bel Air Impala Sport Coupe is shown with optional spinner wheel covers. V-8 prices for this model started at $2,841 while the six-cylinder models started at $2,724. Overall length for this model was 209.1 inches.

# 1958: Flashy new Impala has its grand debut

Chevrolet entered the 1958 model year with an all-new car and an attitude. The facelifted 1957 model had failed to outsell Ford for the first time since 1935 and that was a totally unacceptable situation. Under no circumstances would this be repeated without a battle.

Several factors were at play in 1958, including a recession that had begun in the middle of 1957 and was destined to adversely affect car sales. An expected benefit to Chevrolet would be the natural inclination of buyers to go down-market in times of economic uncertainty. Products in the middle price field, which had been hot in recent years, were destined to suffer in the deepening recession. Some of those folks who had upgraded to the Buick Special, Oldsmobile 88 or

Chrysler Windsor would be returning to the "low-priced three". Others would pass on the "low-priced-three" to try the redesigned American Motors Rambler or any of a raft of European economy cars like the odd Volkswagen, the cute Renault Dauphine, and several sizes of Fiats and Simcas and some quirky British Saloons. Gas was dirt cheap but a surprising portion of the recession stricken public elected, over the next few years, to trade-in nearly new American V-8s, along with a pile of money, to save a couple of bucks a week driving a 36-horsepower throwback to the 1930s that didn't even have a gas gauge and required constant shifting. Honest, it really happened. In all fairness, however, many of those defections were based on the shocking lack of quality control that characterized a large portion of the American auto industry in the mid-to-late 1950s. A good VW was thought to be better than a bad Packard.

Chevrolet for 1958 was billed as "A car that beautifully captures the flair of contemporary living. Lower and longer, wider and stronger. Deep-down new from road to roof ... in styling ... in power ... in ride. Truly a great step forward in motoring!" Some hyperbole there to be sure, but the 1958 Chevrolet was definitely an important step forward. For the second time in three years, a completely new chassis supported Chevys. The new chassis eliminated the center portions of the side rails while beefing up the former X-brace to support the entire mid-section. The new frame was claimed to be 30 percent more rigid

A V-8 Bel Air Convertible is seen with the top down and boot in place. This was known as model 1867. A six-cylinder, model 1767, was also available.

and the open areas at the side made it possible to lower the floors. Incorporated in the new frame was "Full Coil" suspension. The new four-link rear suspension was claimed to restrict rear-end lift and squat for a level ride. For those who demanded an even smoother ride, Chevrolet offered a completely new option, Level Air Suspension. Priced at $124, Level Air employed an engine-driven compressor to supply air bellows, which replaced each of the coil springs. The system took in outside air through an air cleaner and passed it through an anti-icing unit to the air compressor. The compressor fed a high pressure storage tank which was connected by air lines to air springs consisting of bellows and reservoir assembles which replaced the metal springs at each wheel. Level Air was designed to sense changes in passenger or cargo load and make automatic leveling adjustments to keep car height constant and maintain full suspension clearance.

Up front "Ball-Race" steering design was said to reduce steering effort and faster response was the benefit claimed for the new forward mounted steering linkage. Power steering, of course, continued to offer the ultimate in "effortless" steering at a cost of just $70. The pull-type parking brake handle, in use since 1949, was replaced by a new foot-operated parking brake with a suspended release handle to "make parking brake operation quicker and easier." Road wheels employed 11-inch Jumbo-Drum brakes with bonded linings for long life. The reduced effort of vacuum power assist was available at a cost of $38.

This new 1958 Chevrolet was a bigger car with the wheelbase stretched form 115 to 117.5 inches and overall length jumped from 200 to 209.1 inches. Predictably, using the Bel Air four-door sedan as an example, the weight jumped almost 200 pounds. The new bodies were even heavy looking. The deep rear quarter sculpturing, the broad, low grille, wide fender tops and other styling elements gave the new car a very solid look. This was true of all models, especially the new Bel Air Impalas. Available as a sport coupe or convertible, the two Impala models were positioned as premium offerings at the top end of the Bel Air series. While exactly the same length as the Bel Air Sport Coupe, the Impala's unique, low roofline contributed to an illusion of greater length. The Impala Sport Coupe added a simulated air exhaust centered over the backlight and both Impalas, coupe and convertible, had rear fender simulated air scoops, fluted rocker panel moldings, Impala emblems and scripts, specific two-tone break and triple taillight group incorporating a clear backup light lens which replaced the two lamp unit of other coupes and sedans. Impalas and all other 1958 Chevrolets featured the popular new dual headlights to "extend road visibility at night for safer driving." Impalas were blessed with seven very contemporary interior trims consisting of tri-toned striped material in which the broad bands of color were used with harmonizing shades of vinyl. The door panels featured a unique, long armrest incorporating a safety reflector and tinted bands of anodized aluminum. The sport coupe's rear seat center

**A proposed 1958 Delray two-door sedan is shown in the styling courtyard on July 27, 1956. Note the proposed deck lid ornamentation, which included a crest and a V. In production the crest was replaced by a "Chevrolet" script.**

"hideaway" armrest, instead of folding out of the seatback, rose from the seat cushion and could be retracted to accommodate a center passenger. Front seats featured chrome end panels on both cushion and backrest. The Impala steering wheel was a specific unit with two perforated spokes and the Impala crest centered at the hub. Impala convertible tops were now supplied in six colors. The familiar black and white (called ivory) offerings were joined by cream, light gray, light blue and light green. Buyers could choose from at least two top colors, up to three in many cases, with any exterior color. Something for nothing is a concept seldom found in the business world and that was true in 1958. This new top-of-the-line Chevrolet, in eight-cylinder form, had an advertised delivered price of $2,693 for the sport coupe and $2,841 for the convertible. In 1957 the best eight-cylinder sport coupe and convertible were priced at $2,304 and $2,611, respectively.

The standard garden-variety Bel Air was available in four body styles: Sport Coupe, two-door sedan, Sport Sedan and four-door sedan. While lacking the Impala's added ornamentation and unique roofline, the Bel Air was still a well-trimmed car that was, possibly, more appealing to the traditional Chevrolet buyer than the sleek Impala. The body-length side moldings, described as "spear-type" in the dealer album, featured a series of horizontal ribs on the front fender and dual parallel strips on the doors and quarter. A ribbed rear roof pillar applique was used on both two-door models and the Sport Sedan, while a smooth bright applique was employed by the four-door sedan which, along with the two-door sedan, also boasted upper door moldings. Front fender ornaments were perched atop the broad front fenders, four bright inserts known as "front fender accent moldings" filled the angled fender "has mark" depressions. These moldings were balanced by four small vertical moldings on the rear quarter panel windsplits. All Bel Airs featured full wheel discs.

The Bel Air interior was highlighted by seats upholstered in any of six combinations of three tone Jacquard weave pattern cloth and vinyl fabrics. Foam rubber seat cushions were found front and rear. Deep pile rayon floor carpeting covered the floors. The colors established in the seat fabrics were carried over to the door trim panels and rear sidewalls which were trimmed with bright moldings and featured long, separately applied armrests. A horizontal recess running the entire width of the instrument panel was filled with a bright edged trim plate. The standard electric clock was at the far right. The new, deep-hub, two-spoke steering wheel featured a horn ring and a large decorative center applique. The parking brake was now foot operated.

The new Biscayne line was slotted just below the Bel Air, replacing the 210 of 1957. While less glittery than the Bel Air, the Biscayne two-door and four-door post sedans still had the curb appeal of a more expensive car with a full body length spear molding with insert area. The greenhouse area benefited from

A line of recently completed 1958 Chevrolets outside a California plant. Two V-8 Impala Sport Coupes, a six-cylinder Brookwood wagon and a Bel Air four-door sedan are shown.

bright side window reveal moldings as well as windshield and backlight moldings. The "gull-wing" sculptured upper rear quarter panel character line, like that of the Bel Air, was highlighted by a bright molding which swept down to enclose the taillights. Biscayne buyers who preferred wheel covers paid extra to replace the standard hubcaps. The front fender ornaments were also extra-cost accessories for Biscayne. Other Bel Air jewelry including the front fender accent moldings, quarter panel windsplit moldings, and rear roof pillar bright appliques was not available to Biscayne buyers.

Biscayne interiors, while lacking some of the Bel Air luxury touches, had their own measure of period fashion. Five three-tone vinyl and nylon-rayon pattern cloth interiors were offered. Notable differences included the Biscayne's use of vinyl-coated rubber carpeting, deletion of bright moldings on door and sidewall trim and deletion of the full-width bright instrument panel trim plate. Seat design was simplified and Biscayne did not share Bel Air's rear foam rubber cushion although a foam rubber front cushion was standard. Like Bel Air models, Biscayne's center glove compartment was lockable and featured an automatic light.

Chevrolet's entry-level series for 1958 was the Delray, which replaced the 150 series of 1957. The Delray was available in three models, four-door sedan, two-door sedan and two-door utility sedan. While not as grimly plain as base models of as recent as 1955,

the Delray was far from glitzy. The exterior was basically that of the Biscayne with a few items deleted. The window reveal moldings which gave the Biscayne the look of a hardtop disappeared, as did the lower portion of the body side moldings.

Delray buyers were spared the chore of choosing an interior. The only available interior was gunmetal and silver cloth and vinyl. Actually, the gunmetal was dark enough to appear black. A horizontally ribbed charcoal nylon-rayon pattern cloth was used in the seating surfaces with bolsters of silver vinyl. The door trim panels and sidewalls were in silver and black vinyl. Door panel, sidewalls and upper seat bolsters were accented with large rectangular embossments, which added a measure of style to the otherwise severe environment. The washable black rubber floor carpet was embossed in a contemporary design, which complimented the other interior design elements. The utility sedan was essentially the two-door sedan, a low platform replacing the rear seat to form a 31-cubic-foot load compartment. Plain rear sidewall trim replaced the sedans embossed trim and the rear window regulator was eliminated in favor of fixed glass. Armrests were considered extra-cost accessories on Delrays, as was the right side sunvisor. Unlike that of the other Chevrolets for 1958, the Delray's new steering wheel did not incorporate a horn ring, utilizing, instead, a horn button. Other Biscayne standard features that were deleted with the Delray trim level were: glove compartment light, chrome-

This is a 1958 Bel Air Sport Sedan, a V-8 model 1839. That large ribbed front fender molding and the four vertical moldings on the rear quarter panel windsplit were exclusive to Bel Air models.

capped control knobs, cigarette lighter, rear ashtray and front door light switches.

Some of Chevrolet's design, comfort, and convenience features for 1958 were common to all models from the Delray through the Impala; the fuel filler was relocated behind a door in the panel between the bumper and the decklid. The lower corners of the windshield were pulled back for a more extreme wrap-around. All sedan and coupe backlights (rear windshields) were similarly wrapped. Chevrolet's one-key lock system offered the convenience of using one key to operate the entire vehicle's locks. Safety Plate glass was used in all windows. Outside air was drawn in through a full-width cowl ventilation inlet. The center area of front and rear bumpers featured a raised rail with simulated integral bumper guards. The license plates mounted on anodized aluminum facias recessed between the simulated guards. This would become a Chevrolet styling trademark for the better part of a decade.

Station wagons were not officially attached to the passenger car series. Although the station wagon trim levels corresponded almost exactly to Bel Air, Biscayne and Delray trim levels, they were merchandised under their own unique names. Here's how it worked; the top-of-the-line Nomad was four-door six-passenger using Bel Air exterior and interior trim. The Brookwood was a four-door available in six-passenger or nine-passenger configurations sharing the Biscayne exterior and interior trim. The Yeoman six-

passenger wagon shared the Delray trim level but substituted a more durable vinyl for cloth in seating surfaces. The Yeoman could be had in either two-door or four-door configuration. The Yeoman was now Chevrolet's only two-door wagon, corresponding models from the 1957 210 and Bel Air line didn't make the cut for 1958. The Nomad name was now being used by a rather conventional four-door wagon and the beautiful, if less practical two-door Nomad was history.

These new wagons were definitely more functional than their predecessors. For example, the Yeoman four-door was nine inches longer, nearly two inches lower and almost four inches wider than the comparable 1957 model. Cargo space was increased to 88 cubic feet. With wider, higher opening tailgates/liftgates it was possible to haul up to a half-ton of bulkier cargo. New link-type tailgate supports were engineered to keep the lower tailgate level with the cargo floor to create an extra-long deck area for better support when hauling longer loads. With slanted pillars and the gracefully sloped rear profile, the new 1958 Chevrolet wagons were less boxy than their predecessors. Greater visibility was afforded by the large curved rear window in the new wraparound upper liftgate, which was also extended into the roof for a taller opening. This tailgate design permitted the loading of taller objects. The upper liftgate was fitted with a separate handle to allow easy opening for loading small objects without lowering the tailgate. Disappearing supports made it possible to lock the

With a base price of $2,155, this Delray was Chevrolet's least expensive four-door sedan. The only visible option on this 3,439-pound vehicle is the two-tone paint.

liftgate in any of seven open positions. With the new wraparound liftgate, the previous wraparound quarter windows were replaced by conventional flat side glass.

As recently as 1949, Chevrolet buyers didn't have to devote much attention to the problem of which engine/transmission would best suit their needs. There was one engine and one transmission. By 1954 the buyers could select a three-speed manual transmission or a Powerglide automatic. Each came with its own version of the 235-cid in-line six-cylinder engine. Probably not a painful decision there either. In 1955 overdrive and several different levels of 265-cid V-8 performance were added to the mix. To satisfy customer demand, the proliferation continued through 1956 and 1957. The ability to personalize the powertrain in the new car continued to be important to the buyers of 1958. To those folks Chevrolet offered an extensive array of economy- or performance-oriented powertrains. The familiar 235-cid Blue-Flame 6 was continued with hydraulic lifters and was rated 145-hp at 4,200 rpm (torque: 215 at 2,400 rpm). It could be combined with a three-speed manual, three-speed with overdrive or a Powerglide two-speed automatic transmission. The base V-8 was now the 283-cid Turbo-Fire two-barrel developing 185 hp at 4,600 rpm (torque: 275 at 2,400). It could be combined with three-speed manual, three-speed with overdrive, Powerglide two-speed automatic, or the Turboglide triple-turbine automatic. The first optional V-8 was the 230 hp at 4,800 rpm (torque: 300 at 3,000) Super

Turbo-Fire V-8, a 283-cid V-8 with four-barrel carb. Transmission choices were identical to those offered with the two-barrel Turbo-Fire. Fuel injection returned in 1958 on the 250 hp at 5,000 rpm (torque: 305 at 3,800) Ramjet 283-cid V-8. Ramjet fuel injection was offered with the three-speed manual transmission or Turboglide automatic. A new family of 348-cid engines was introduced for 1958. The entry level 348 was the four-barrel Turbo-Thrust developing 250 hp at 4,400 rpm (torque: 355 at 2,800 rpm). The Turbo-Thrust could be specified with three-speed manual, Powerglide or Turboglide. The Super Turbo-Thrust 348 was supplied with three two-barrels, developing a very healthy 280 hp at 4,800 rpm (torque: 355 at 3,200 rpm). The three-speed manual and Turboglide were the transmission choices for Super Turbo-Thrust. These same choices were offered when, after introduction, an 11.0:1 compression Super Turbo Thrust with a horsepower rating of 315 at 5,600 rpm was added to the option list.

In 1958 the first generation Corvette received another major facelift. The most significant area of change was the new front end where new quad headlights reigned over a projecting new three-unit grille. Following the excellent 1956-57 design, this new front end was regarded by some (well, at least the author) as guppy-like. The simulated hood louvers, dummy air scoops in the fender coves, and chrome deck lid "suspenders" were not serious contributions to the vehicle billed as "America's only production sports

The new Corvette's simulated hood louvers are clearly shown here. These louvers were exclusive to 1958 Corvettes.

car." Wraparound bumpers afforded better quarter panel protection and incorporated oval exhaust ports.

In the "definitely improved" column was the new instrument panel. The new panel featured a large 160-mph speedometer housed in a pod, which encircled the 6,000-rpm tachometer. A complete set of gauges was arranged at either side of the tachometer, directly in front of the driver. The passenger received a big, much appreciated, grab bar to hold on to, perhaps while praying. A new center console housing the shifter, radio, clock, heater controls and ashtray swept down from the dash to divide the individual bucket seats.

Of course, the Corvette was about much more than appearance and in the really important ride and drive areas (read: handle well and go fast) the 1958 model continued to offer the performance and handling options that made it a world class sports car. In fact, the top performing 10.5:1 compression Ramjet fuel injection 283 ($484) was now rated at 290 hp at 6,200 rpm, up seven horses from the 1957 version. Three other 283 engines could be specified. The base four-barrel developed 230 hp at 4,800 rpm, with two four-barrels ($150) the rating jumped to 245 hp at 5,000 rpm. A special cam version of the 283 with two four-barrels offered 270 hp at 6,000 rpm and the milder cam, 9.5:1 compression Ramjet fuel injection 283 ($484) produced 250 hp at 500 rpm. If the buyer was really serious about all-out driving, heavy-duty brakes and suspension ($780.10), four-speed manual transmission ($215), Positraction ($48.45), and various axle ratios were readily available. If he or she just

wanted to look good, Powerglide ($188), heater ($97), signal-seeking AM radio ($144), whitewalls ($31.65), power top ($140) helped ease the brutal realities of sports car ownership.

It was in 1958 that Corvette's closest competitor disappeared. Ford's two-passenger thunderbird, which had been marketed from the beginning as a "personal car," became a four-passenger coupe or convertible. It was a win-win situation that resulted in both Ford and Chevrolet being virtually alone in their own little market niche. The Corvette was now generally acknowledged to be "America's only production sports car." Thunderbird finally found happiness cast in the roll of a high-style darling of the somewhat-to-very-wealthy set as an alternative to the traditional luxury car. Such a deal.

Ford continued, in 1958, to be the real competition for Chevrolet's passenger cars. While the hot selling (number one in sales) 1957 Fords were generally regarded as stylish cars, few would accuse the facelifted 1958 Fords of being the prettiest cars on the block. The new front end, incorporating the popular quad headlights, looked blunt, heavy, and clumsy. The rear treatment was frequently singled out for criticism. The four oval taillights were an unwelcome (and temporary) departure from the trademark round units. The deck lid with a depressed center section was not as attractive as the unit it replaced. All coupes and sedans were treated to front-to-rear ribbed roofs.

The new Bel Air Sport Coupe took a back seat to the Impala. A bright ribbed C-pillar was added but the Impala's unique rear quarter panel simulated air scoop, rocker molding and crossed flags emblem were not used.

The entry-level Custom series of 1957 was dropped, leaving the Custom 300 to serve as the base series. There were several different exterior trim packages offered for the Custom exterior which could make the vehicle's appearance range from rather stark to fairly flashy. In the base trim level the Custom 300 of 1958 was visually closer to the previous year's base Custom than to the 1957 Custom 300. These 116-inch wheelbase vehicles were offered in two-door sedan, four-door sedan and business couple models. With three models ranging from $1,977 to $2,119 (six-cylinder) the Custom 300 was targeted directly at the 117.5-inch wheelbase Chevrolet Delray series (six-cylinder) which was priced at $2,013 to $2,155. When the available interior and exterior trim packages were added in the Custom 300, the price spread could rise closer to that of the Chevrolet Biscayne series whose six-cylinder models were priced at $2,236 and $2,290.

The Delray at 209.1 inches was 7.1 inches longer than the Custom 300 and had a significantly longer rear overhang but was exactly the same height and fractions narrower. Surprisingly, the Chevrolet enjoyed a significantly large (over six feet) advantage in wall-to-wall turning diameter. Using four-door sedans as our basis of comparison, Chevrolet enjoyed slight advantages in front and rear headroom and more noteworthy advantages in front legroom, and front and rear hip room. The Custom 300 enjoyed the advantage in front and rear shoulder room only. The Delray weighed 187 pounds more than the Custom 300.

The 118-inch wheelbase Fairlane and Fairlane 500 were continued for 1958. All closed models were available as pillared or pillarless models. With prices (six-cylinder) ranging from $2,198 to $2,394, the Fairlane also competed with the Chevrolet Biscayne. Actually Ford enjoyed an advantage over Chevrolet in the pricing of the entry level two-door hardtop at $2,329 for the six-cylinder Fairlane Club Victoria ($2,453 for the V-8) compared to Chevrolet's entry level six-cylinder Bel Air Sport Coupe at $2,447 ($2,554). The Bel Air, of course, provided a much better trim level than that of the Fairlane but the entry level hardtop buyer could save about $118 buying a Ford and more than 16,000 buyers did just that. The Fairlane 500 shared the long wheelbase and bigger body of the Fairlane while adding upscale interior and exterior trim. The base Fairlane was easily identified by a side trim treatment in which bright moldings flowed back from the leading edge of the front fenders, tapering to a point just ahead of the rear wheel opening. This simulated cove area was painted the top color on two-tone vehicles. The Fairlane 500 utilized a front-to-rear molding ensemble with a gold anodized metal insert. The Fairlane 500 series was host to the Skyliner retractable hardtop, the innovative but somewhat impractical and expensive alternative to the traditional convertible. The convertible coupe was also unique to the Fairlane 500 series. The Fairlane's wheelbase was almost one inch longer than that of the Chevrolet but Chevrolet was better than two inches longer overall. Ford was 28 pounds heavier in base

The 1958 Corvette featured a new instrument panel with this center console featuring ventilation, temperature, defroster, and radio controls, plus an electric clock. The optional signal-seeking Wonderbar radio and the selector for the optional Powerglide are shown.

trim. Chevrolet's advantage in wall-to-wall turning diameter over the Fairlane models increased to 5.68 feet. Chevrolet also enjoyed interior roominess advantages over the Fairlane sedans in front and rear head room, front and rear leg room and front and rear hip room. Ford had a thin lead in front and rear shoulder room.

While 1958 was a year of economy concerns, the horsepower race was still raging. Ford's base engine was still the economical OHV in-line 6 rated at 145 hp. The base V-8 was the 205 hp 292 cid two-barrel. The next step was to the 240-hp, 332-cid four-barrel V-8. When a four-barrel was added, the horsepower jumped to 265. Ford's biggest engine for 1958 was the 352-cid four-barrel V-8, which made 300 horsepower at 4,600. The torque rating was 395 at 2,800 rpm. For the record, Ford's base V-8 and largest optional V-8 both carried higher horsepower ratings than the comparable Chevrolet engines.

Ford, of course, called itself the "wagonmaster," and with some justification. For 1958 two two-door wagons and four four-door wagons were offered. At entry level, the Ranch Wagon buyer could select from two-door or four-door models. The Del Rio Ranch Wagon which had been Ford's two-door competition to the now defunct premium level two-door Nomad, was continued. The four-door Country Sedan was offered in both six and nine-passenger models. At the top of the line the nine-passenger Country Sedan continued to be the only woodgrained wagon in its class. It was the

exclusive woodgrained treatment that gave Ford the edge with many wagon buyers of the era. Like Chevrolet, Ford wagons featured a liftgate/tailgate design. Chevrolet's big advantage was the second seat design, which enabled one-operation folding contrasted to Ford's rather clumsy design that required a series of operations. Chevrolet also enjoyed dimensional advantages in the cargo area including up to 7.9 inches in load-space length and 4.5 inches greater width between wheelhouses.

Plymouth, which had been a very hot car with awful quality in 1957, made very few important visual changes for 1958. The highly prized cone shape covers, many of which found their way onto 1957 Chevrolets, were replaced by a flatter design. The popular quad headlamps and a new lower valance panel gave a new look up front. The tall blade taillights gave way to round units, which went in the place where the backup lights had been in 1957, while a pair of thin bright moldings replaced the taillights. Side trim for the Belvedere was revised to the shape established by the 1957 Fury. The important changes were mostly unseen. Those were the redesign of components that had caused so much trouble in 1957. While quality at Chrysler Corporation was improved across the board, the test of time would still find the 1958 Chevrolet to be of superior quality to the Plymouth. While the Plymouth's wheelbase was a half-inch greater, Chevrolet was 3.1 inches longer overall. Plymouth was wider by almost two inches and lower by one-half inch.

The sporty two-door Nomad was gone but this 1958 four-door Nomad six-passenger did a much better job serving America's families. The wide roof moldings and the belt molding (just visible at the bottom of the windows) were Nomad exclusives.

Chevrolet's Delray four-door outweighed the comparable Plymouth Plaza by more than 160 pounds.

Plymouth was offered in four series: The Plaza, Savoy, Belvedere and the performance-oriented, low-volume Fury. The standard Fury was powered by a hot 318 V-8 with two four-barrel carburetors, which made 290 hp at 5,200 rpm. All Plymouths were available with the Golden Commando 350-cubic-inch V-8, also featuring a pair of four-barrel carburetors, which developed 305 horses at 5,000 rpm. That same 350 powerplant, when teamed with fuel injection, was rated at 315 hp at 5,000 rpm. Few of these fuel-injected units made it out the door and most were field converted to two four-barrels by Chrysler technicians who couldn't make the temperamental things behave. Seems that the electronic controls were receiving stray signals from similar, but more powerful units, on large trucks. Imagine if you will, cruising a crowded freeway in your 315-hp car, which suddenly receives a "let's go" message from a nearby 18-wheeler and goes into full acceleration mode. Scary. This was the type of quality glitch that made the silly looking Volkswagen look a lot better.

Plymouth's station wagons were offered in two-door and four-door versions with some features, which distinguished them from Chevrolet and Ford offerings. Plymouth's roll-down tailgate window eventually became the industry standard. The Plymouth rear-facing third seat was well padded but not a favorite of those who didn't like riding backwards.

1958 was the year that American Motors caught the public's attention. The 1956 and 1957 Ramblers were a little two quirky for most folks, although the peppy little V-8 Rebel attracted a few rabid enthusiasts. For 1958 the basic unitized body got a very extensive facelift, which included a massive diecast grille and some very angular lines. This facelift was an instant success and many of the newly practical minded buyers of 1958 found the Rambler fit their needs perfectly. At the low end, the Rambler Six Deluxe was just a bit more than $100 below the Chevrolet Delray. It would haul the same six passengers in a vehicle that was a foot and a half shorter, 5.5 inches narrower and 650 pounds lighter. It was easier to drive with standard steering, easier to park and used less gas. The upright Rambler boasted better front and rear headroom and front and rear shoulder room while falling short in legroom and hiproom. A 1958 Delray six stick with manual steering and manual brakes was not really much fun to drive through rush hour traffic and park in a tight spot. The Rambler, while not a sports car, was a pretty nice little driver and didn't need to be manhandled into a parking space.

AMC caught the eye of the public with a strange but low risk move; the not-at-all-new Rambler American. Back in 1956, when the new 108" wheelbase Rambler arrived, the original 100-inch wheelbase model was retired. Well, for 1958, AMC dusted off the dies, changed the rear wheel openings and grille, and there it was; the 100" wheelbase

A 1958 Corvette is shown bouncing over the Belgian road course at the GM Proving Ground in Milford, Michigan. This Corvette was wearing the removable plastic hardtop.

Rambler American. Surprisingly, the modest changes worked and the American was a pretty nice little car for almost $500 less than the Biscayne. It wasn't competitive on a head-to-head basis but, again, the Delray had grown to become more car than some people wanted, and for those buyers, the American was worth a look.

While not a good year for the industry in general, 1958 was less of a disaster for Chevrolet than it as for Ford, Plymouth and most of the industry. With total sales of 1,216,597 regular Chevrolets compared to 950,053 Fords (does not include 37,892 Thunderbirds) Chevrolet was clearly back in the driver's seat. In fact, Chevrolet's percentage of the industry increased from 25 to 29.59 percent. Of course, there were those pesky imports and the newly bold American Motors stirring up the mud at the bottom of the market. AMC's percentage of industry production doubled in 1958 and its position in industry sales went from 12th place to 10th. And the imports? Well, by the end of 1958 more than 220,000 VWs were on the roads of the U.S. and two newcomers called Toyopet and Datsun were starting to trickle in from Japan. Overpriced, undersized, underpowered and burdened with funny names and strange styling they were certainly destined to be no more than blips on the screen.

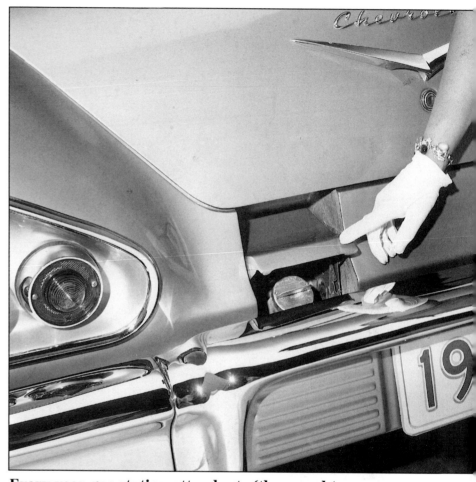

**Every year gas station attendants (they used to pump your gas!) had to find out where Chevrolet had hidden the fuel filler. In 1958 it was found behind an access door just inboard of the left taillight.**

**'58**

This dramatic shot shows the differences in rear end design between the new 1958 Impala and the 1957 Bel Air. This angle clearly displays the new ribbed and anodized license plate panel.

This 1958 Delray two-door sedan was Chevrolet's least expensive six-passenger car. This one was a completely base six-cylinder, model 1141 (a V-8 would be model 1241) which carried an advertised price of $2,101.

A gleaming new two-tone mid-level Biscayne V-8 two-door sedan gets a critical eye in the final inspection area before entering the world. This was a model 1641 weighing 3,407 pounds.

Model 1694 was the V-8 version of Chevrolet's only nine-passenger wagon, a four-door Brookwood. Remember the rolled up jeans?

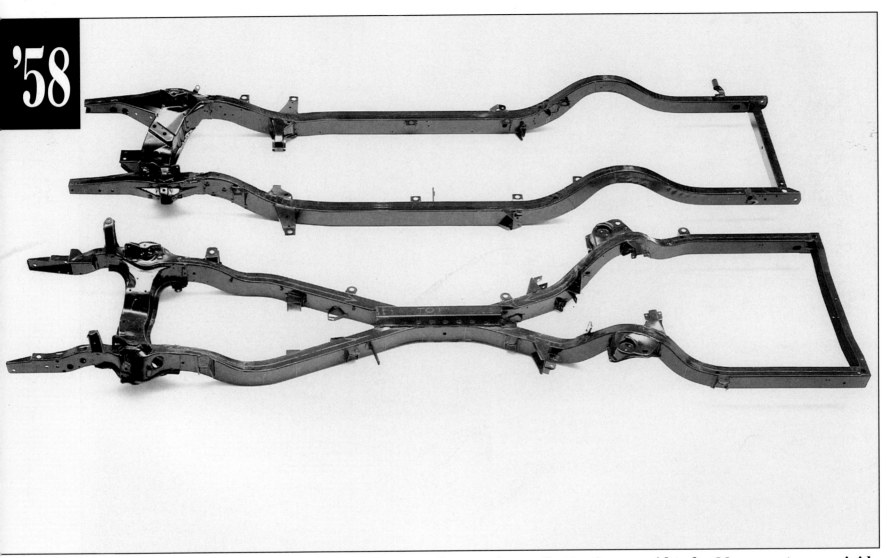

Here's a comparison of the new and old frames. The new frame (bottom) was said to be 30 percent more rigid. This design allowed the deep rear foot wheels. Note the attachment points for the new rear coil springs.

This proving ground shot shows the familiar Blue Flame 6 in the new surroundings of a 1958 Chevrolet engine bay. This engine is now rated at 145 hp.

A might-have-been proposal for the 1958 front end shows the grille mounted V with an integral crest below a humongous "Chevrolet" script on the hood. A centered hood ornament and longitudinally ribbed headliner were proposed.

The Impala Sport Coupe featured this colorful interior with tri-toned nylon-faced Jacquard-weave striped pattern cloth and leather-grain vinyl. The "hideaway" rear center armrest could be collapsed to seat cushion level to provide a center seating position.

This is an early clay mock-up version of the right rear fender manual antenna, part no. 987733, that sold, in slightly modified form, for $7.65.

The 1958 Nomad was easily identified by the bright strips (seven of them) on the tailgate. The wraparound liftgate greatly increased the width of the opening above the belt. This V-8 carried an advertised price of $2,835.

With extra cost two-tone paint, whitewalls and California dealer plate, this 1958 Biscayne two-door sedan shows the standard upper window moldings that contribute to the "hardtop" look. A V-8 model 1641, it weighs 3,407 pounds.

The dual headlamps were new this year and standard for all models. A Bel Air is shown, identified by the four angled front fender ornaments, which replaced the 1957 hood rockets.

Considering that this six-cylinder Delray was Chevrolet's least expensive four-door sedan, and that the only visible option is two-tone paint, it is evident that base models had come a long way in the years since 1955. This is model 1149 with an advertised price of just $2,155.

MADLER
11-30-55

12417

This clay model, shot on November 30, 1955, shows that the three-piece window that sunk the 1957 Buick and Olds was under consideration for the 1958 Chevrolet Sport Sedan. The rear bumper treatment, which incorporated an exhaust port, was interesting.

The V-8 Impala Convertible model 1867 is shown in a rear view with the top up. This top was offered in six colors.

**Chevrolet was still very committed to the All-American Soap Box Derby in 1958. This 1958 Impala Convertible was an official car at Derby Downs in Akron, Ohio on August 17, 1958.**

The Impala is quickly identified by triple-unit taillights, the ribbed rocker molding and the simulated air exhaust on the rear quarter panel. The roof mounted simulated air exhaust is barely visible in this shot.

**'58**

A 1958 Corvette with the plastic removable hardtop kicks up a little dust at Milford. The new front end treatment featured twin dual headlamps and retained the toothy grille.

The open door reveals the wide red plastic reflectors mounted in the ends of Impala front door armrests. Also shown are the bright front seat end panel and the tinted aluminum panel surrounding the armrest.

The Bel Air Sport Coupe interior was probably more appealing than that of the Impala to the more traditional, older buyer. Seat inserts were tastefully done in nylon-faced Jacquard-weave diamond design pattern cloth.

This full-size clay model was shot six days before Christmas in 1955. Below the belt the sheet metal was starting to approach the actual design but the C-pillar more closely resembled that of a 1957 Sport Sedan. The bumper is close to the 1957 version and the grille bar and teeth show Corvette influence.

**'58**

The new "X" frame provided room for the recessed rear foot wells seen at either side of the tailpipes. The new rear coil suspension is also shown.

Those of us who have tried to travel in a trunk-less third generation Corvette can only view with envy the wonderfully spacious and well-trimmed luggage compartment of the 1959 Corvette.

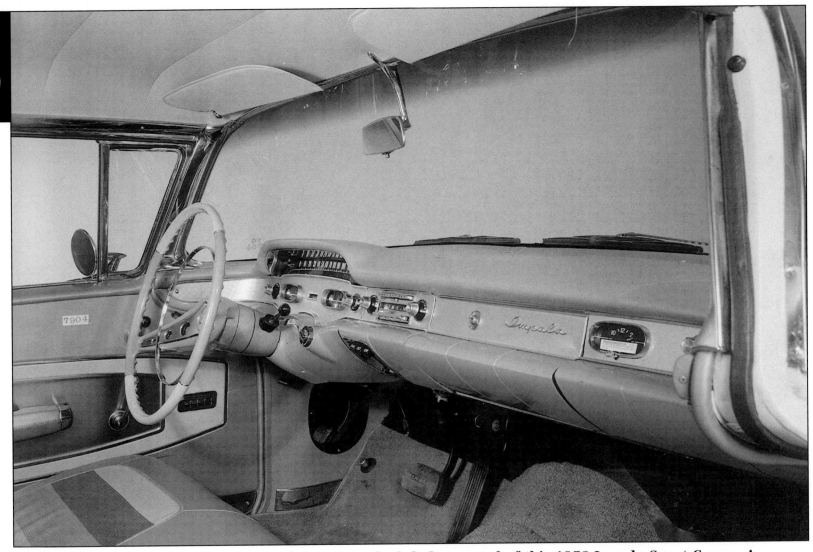

The master power window switch can be seen on the left door panel of this 1958 Impala Sport Coupe. A Wonderbar radio is shown. That two-tone sport-type steering wheel was exclusive to Impalas.

This is the new 250 hp Turbo-Thrust V-8. The 348 four-barrel was a bargain option at $59 over the 283 two-barrel. This vehicle also had power brakes and power steering. The generator drove the steering pump.

This 1958 Impala Sport Coupe mock-up is a wealth of incorrect ornamentation. The crest was not used on V-8 decklids, the Impala script was not used on the rear, those bumper guards didn't make it but the exhaust ports were offered as an accessory. They sold for $8.90 a pair.

A sturdy rubber mat covered the trunk floor of the 1958 Impala convertible. The cardboard liner can be seen at the left and the jacking instructions are on the inside of the deck lid.

The 1958 V-8 Bel Air four-door sedan was described as possessing "thin pillars" and it did resemble a four-door hardtop with the window frame moldings and C-pillar molding. This model is 1849. Chevrolet proudly noted that it was more than nine inches longer and almost four inches wider than ever before.

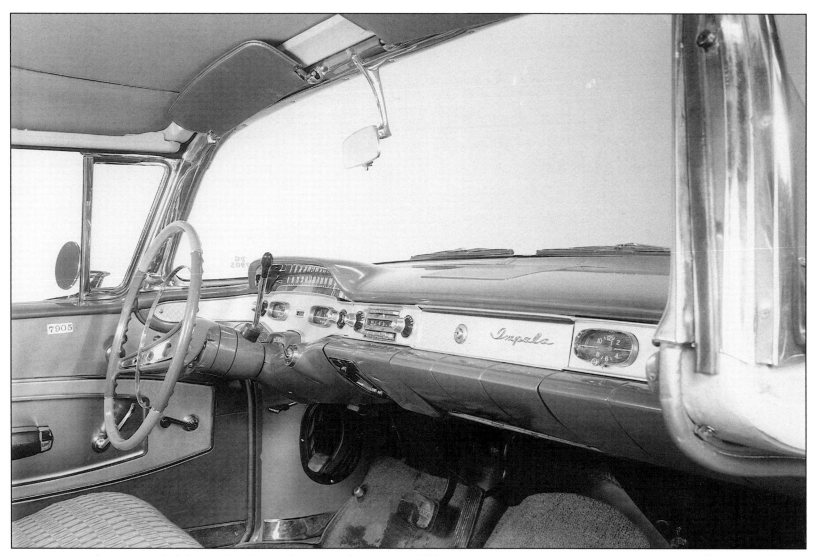

To protect the seat of this 1958 Chevrolet Impala convertible test car, a seat cover has been installed. The light area on the instrument panel is a silver textured trim plate used only on Bel Air series vehicles. The parking brake release can be seen under the left end of the panel.

Chevrolet's least expensive 1958 station wagon was this six-cylinder Yeoman two-door, six-passenger, model 1191. In this totally base condition, it carried an advertised price of $2,413.

Officially a member of the Delray family, this sedan delivery shows its one-piece liftgate. Known as model 1171 (6) or 1271 (V-8), the sedan delivery was a favorite of owner-drivers.

TRENT
12·29·55

The woods are full of folks who didn't like the 1958 restyle of the Corvette. Well it could have been worse. Shot in the Styling Dome on December 29, 1955, this clay proposal for the 1958 Corvette is shown with a new 1956 Thunderbird.

TRENT
12-29-55

12694

The car in the center is a 1958 Corvette clay model bracketed by a 1956 Thunderbird and a 1955 Mercedes Gullwing. The Corvette roof shows Gullwing door cut lines. The split window eventually showed up in 1963.

**With three two-barrel carburetors, this 348-cid Super Turbo-Thrust V-8 had a 9.5:1 compression ratio and developed 280 hp.**

This two-tone V-8 Biscayne four-door sedan was model 1649. The parallel moldings on fenders and doors formed an area filled by anodized inserts. Bright upper door moldings added to the well-dressed look.

Level Air Suspension was introduced in 1958. It incorporated an air spring at each wheel. It was intended to improve riding qualities and also keep the car level, regardless of load.

The Bel Air V-8 four-door sedan had a base advertised price of $2,547, $71 less than the four-door hardtop version, the Bel Air Sport Sedan. At 3,470 pounds, it was also lighter by 44 pounds.

The radical wraparound windshield of the 1958 Chevrolet offered no place to mount the traditional spotlight. This study by Chevrolet Engineering is fairly close to the accessory spotlight that was ultimately offered.

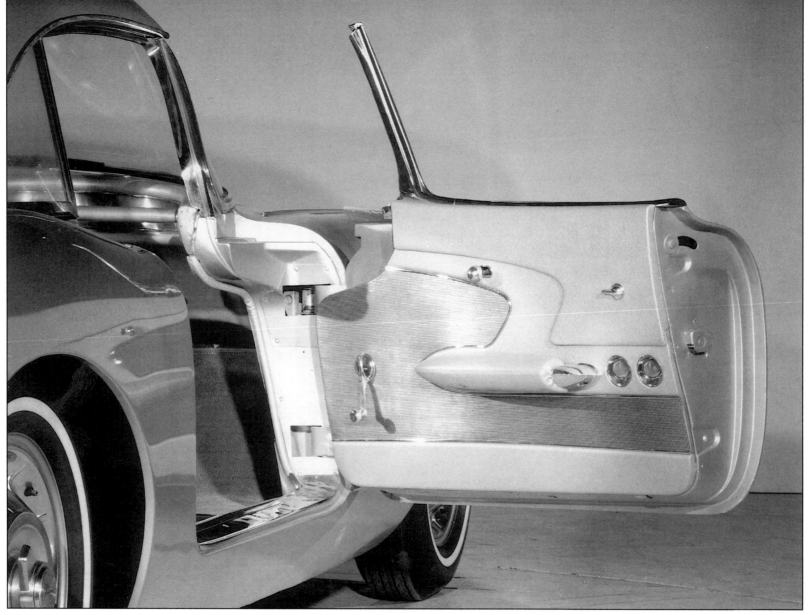

The Corvette door trim panel was obviously an expensive item to produce. The bright area on the door was a tinted anodized aluminum panel. Two safety reflectors were used in each door.

A 1958 Bel Air Sport Coupe moves up into the fast lane of the high-speed track at GM's Milford Proving Ground. It shares the track with several Cameo Carriers.

The Delray sedan delivery had a wide door opening and a flat cargo floor. At $2,123, the six-cylinder version was $290 less than the two-door Yeoman wagon.

An Impala Sport Coupe body is about to be mated to its 348-equipped chassis. The deck lid's torsion bars are seen at this angle.

A bird's-eye view shows the tri-tone pattern vinyl interior. The optional rear seat speaker is mounted behind the grille recessed in the rear seat back.

**'58**

A two-Chevy family gloats over their Biscayne V-8 four-door sedan and their Bel Air Sport Sedan. Carefully study the two-tone color break on the front fender. A short molding above the wheel opening separated the colors.

The angle of this 1958 Impala V-8 convertible shows the concave, textured portion of the grille between the horizontal bars.

This angle of an Impala Sport Coupe clearly shows the simulated air exhaust faired into the roof panel. This V-8 model 1847 weighed 3,459 pounds.

The rear passenger compartment of a Biscayne four-door sedan shows the nylon-faced basket weave design pattern cloth used in these models. The seat bolsters and door panels were vinyl. Floor covering was vinyl-coated rubber carpeting.

The 3/4-rear view of an Impala convertible shows the recessed center, color-keyed body side molding on the door and quarter panel.

A 1958 Impala Sport Coupe in a very modernistic California setting. This V-8 is a model 1847. The full wheel covers were standard and carried an embossed crossed flags emblem.

This Nomad shows off some Chevrolet wagon features. Notice the heavy upper and lower tailgate supports. The upper portion of the gate curves into the sides to provide a very wide opening and the lower gate opens flat to support long cargo or the weight of a person.

With just two options showing, two-tone paint and whitewalls, the entry-level Delray two-door sedan was a good-looking car with clean lines. At 209.1 inches overall, it was also a big car.

How do we know that this rear view shows a Bel Air? The two-tone paint scheme is the giveaway. Note that the lighter color fills the cove area above the taillight as well as half of the area under the taillight. That treatment was unique to the Bel Air trim level. This is a V-8 four-door sedan, model 1849.

When looking at a Bel Air Sport Sedan from this angle, we can see the wide moldings that cap the side windows as well as the way in which the front fenders rise above the hood, which tapers down for excellent forward visibility.

**'58**

The bright seat end caps lent a quality touch to the Impala interior. Notice the roll at the top of the seat back. The bright sill plates can also be seen.

Nearly all photos of 1958 Chevrolet Biscaynes show the base hubcaps, not the optional full wheel covers, which greatly improve the appearance. The author is guessing that this was an official decision to ensure that the nicely decked out Biscayne didn't look good enough to threaten Bel Air sales. This Biscayne V-8 four-door sedan is a model 1649.

The 1958 Corvette interior was, perhaps, too nice for a serious sports car. This interior was certainly the blue-gray color. Features of note are the 140-mph speedometer, 6000-rpm tachometer directly in front of the driver, full complement of gauges, competition-type steering wheel, and passenger-assist bar.

When the judges tell you the jacking instructions on your 1958 Impala are poorly installed, be sure to show them this shot of a brand new Impala taken at the Milford Proving Ground. This shot also shows the routing of the lead for the rear mounted antenna.

This Delray two-door sedan was shot at the vehicle display area of the Dealer Announcement show. It is either a pilot line or very early production model. Note the undercoating in the rear wheel well area. Six-cylinder models used the crest and a "Chevrolet" script on the deck lid. V-8 models gained a V and lost the crest emblem.

The ignition shielding tells us that this Ramjet Fuel Injection 283 is installed in a Corvette. Two levels of fuel injection performance were available for Corvette producing 250 hp or 290 hp.

This fellow is attaching the standard ribbed rocker panel molding to an Impala Sport Coupe. These moldings were an $11.75 option for non-Impalas. Hopefully, the inspectors down the line noticed that the hood blanket is not completely installed. When completed, this V-8 had a base advertised price of $2,693.

The 1958 Corvette received new wraparound bumpers with oval exhaust ports. The new long taillight lenses replaced the former recessed small round units. The new chrome bars on the decklid were destined to be a one-year item, having been the object of more than a little criticism.

An Impala Convertible has been dressed up to display some of the available options. Included are: the door mounted outside rear view mirror, $4.40; non-glare inside rear view mirror, $4.95; right rear fender antenna, $7.65; and a continental wheel carrier, $148 or $137 depending on bumper supplied with car (one piece or three piece). Regrettably, the skirts are not priced in Chevrolet's March 15, 1958 Accessories Confidential Price Schedule.

Looking at this model 1847 Impala V-8 Sport Coupe, it is very difficult to believe that at 209.1 inches overall, it is exactly the same length as the Bel Air Sport Coupe, or any other 1958 Chevrolet Coupe or Sedan. Overall height of 56.4 inches is just 1 inch lower than any other Chevrolet Coupe or Sedan. Unbelievable but true, as the Impala looks much lower and much longer than those other coupes and sedans.

On July 11, 1958, as the model year wound down, this body was married to its chassis in St. Louis. Notice that, due to the Corvette's design, the fenders and body were lowered as a single unit. The rear bumpers were installed at the next station.

The rear interior of a 1958 Biscayne four-door sedan (model 1649 if a V-8 or 1549 if a 6) shows the molded vinyl coated rubber carpeting and the full vinyl seat back and door panels designed for easy cleanup when little muddy feet get careless. A large rear ashtray is centered on the rear seat. The B-pillar is vinyl below the belt, painted metal above.

It's a Bel Air Sport
Coupe, right? Wrong!
This model 1841 V-8
Bel Air two-door
sedan could easily
pass for a hardtop.
With those upper
window moldings it
looked like a hardtop,
had the structural
integrity of a sedan
and cost $61 less than
the sport coupe.

Do real sports cars have whitewalls? According to this shot of three new Corvettes at the St. Louis plant, two out of three do. This shot shows a two-tone Vette with whitewalls, a door mount mirror and a black convertible top. The center car is a very basic single tone with white convertible top. The one on the right has a removable plastic hardtop, door mount mirror, whitewalls and a left rear fender antenna.

The front compartment of a Biscayne four-door sedan shows the steering wheel with horn ring; horizontal speedometer; a non-glare inside rear view mirror, $4.95; a body mount outside rear view mirror, $4.40; a manual radio, $57.25; and the new foot-operated parking brake with finger-tip release.

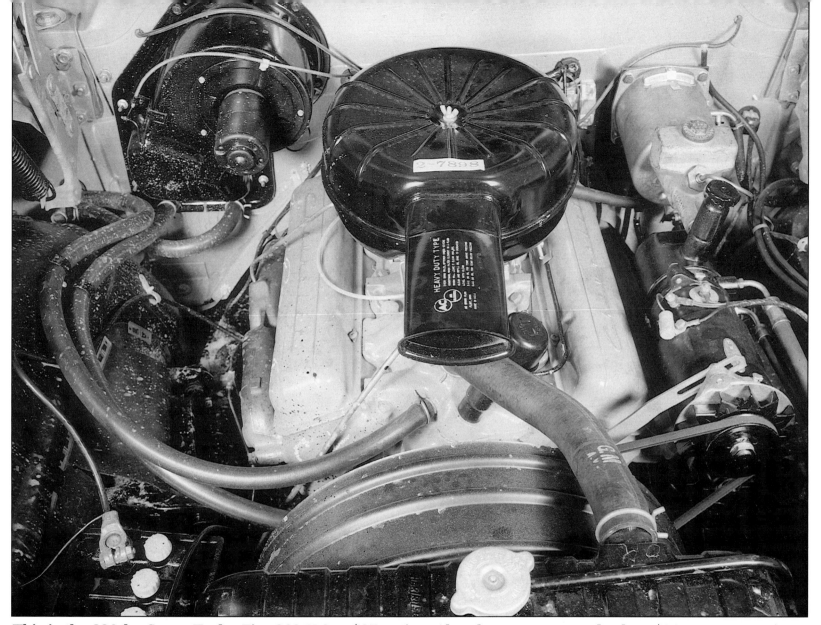

This is the 230-hp Super Turbo-Fire 283 V-8, a $27 option. Also shown are power brakes, $38; power steering, $70; and heater $49.

This is a good angle from which to view the new three-element front-end treatment and simulated hood louver design of the new 1958 Corvette. Note the long moldings filling the front fender valleys from the new headlights to a point just ahead of the windshield.

This is the innocent looking little two-door that took the first big bite out of the American market. It had 36 hp and rode on a 94.5-inch wheelbase. A total of 78,588 of these Volkswagens found new owners in the United States in 1958. This was the first year for the big back window.

Ford abandoned the sports car market in 1958, moving the Thunderbird into a new four-passenger, personal car niche. The decision was a good one with the 1958 Thunderbird nearly doubling the 1957 model's sales.

The French built Renault Dauphine sported a rear engine but, unlike VW, it was water-cooled. It used a three-speed manual transmission. Styling was well received but the quality couldn't begin to touch that of VW (or most anyone else, for that matter).

The anodized trim on the doors and quarter panel identifies this 1958 Ford Custom 300 as one with the styletone package. This 116-inch-wheelbase sedan competed against the Delray, or if well equipped, the Biscayne. This was Ford's second most popular car in 1958.

Plymouth's top of the line 1958 four-door sedan was this Belvedere. While still fielding a nice-looking line of cars, Plymouth sales dropped dramatically this year in response to the multitude and magnitude of 1957 quality flaws.

The 1958 Ford Fairlane 500 Town Victoria was most attractive in profile where the quad taillights and heavy-handed front end design could not be seen. This car featured a 118-inch wheelbase.

At the end of 1955, the little Rambler two-door on a 100-inch wheelbase was phased out. In 1958 the tooling was reassembled, and with modest rear wheel opening and trim changes, it returned as the Rambler American. The base Deluxe model is shown.

An old saying goes like this: "Always leave them laughing." This 1958 Edsel four-door hardtop was in the Pacer series. The costlier of the two Ford based series. The Ranger was base while the bigger, more square Corsair and Citation were Mercury based. This model was priced $210 above a comparable Bel Air Sport Sedan. Consumers couldn't see the added value.

# 1958 CHEVROLET MODEL CHART

| TYPE | BEL AIR | | BISCAYNE | | DELRAY | | WAGONS | |
|---|---|---|---|---|---|---|---|---|
| | 6 CYL. | 8 CYL. | 6 CYL. | 8 CYL. | 6 CYL. | 8 CYL. | 6 CYL. | 8 CYL. |
| 2-Door Sedan | 1741 | 1841 | 1541 | 1641 | 1141 | 1241 | | |
| 2-Door Utility Sedan | | | | | 1121 | 1221 | | |
| 4-Door Sedan | 1749 | 1849 | 1549 | 1649 | 1149 | 1249 | | |
| | | | | | | | | |
| Sport Coupe  (2-dr. hdtp.) | 1731 | 1831 | | | | | | |
| Sport Sedan (4-dr. hdtp.) | 1739 | 1839 | | | | | | |
| | | | | | | | | |
| Impala Sport Coupe (2-dr. hdtp) | 1747 | 1847 | | | | | | |
| Impala Convertible | 1767 | 1867 | | | | | | |
| | | | | | | | | |
| Nomad 4-Door 6-pass. | | | | | | | 1793 | 1893 |
| Brookwood 4-Door 6-pass. | | | | | | | 1593 | 1693 |
| Brookwood 4-Door 9-pass. | | | | | | | 1594 | 1694 |
| Yeoman 4-Door 6-pass. | | | | | | | 1193 | 1293 |
| Yeoman 2-Door 6-pass. | | | | | | | 1191 | 1291 |

# 1958 EXTERIOR SPECIFICATION COMPARISONS OF FOUR-DOOR SEDANS

| | CHEVROLET | FORD CUSTOM 300 | FORD FAIRLANE | PLYMOUTH | RAMBLER 6 |
|---|---|---|---|---|---|
| Wheelbase | 117.5" | 116.03" | 118.04" | 118.0" | 108" |
| Overall Length | 209.1" | 202.0" | 207.0" | 206.0" | 191.15" |
| Front Overhang | 35.8" | 34.95" | 34.95" | 32.8" | 32.0" |
| Rear Overhang | 55.8" | 51.01" | 59.0" | 55.2" | 51.2" |
| Height (design load) | 57.1" | 57.1" | 56.2" | 56.6" | 58.0" |
| Width | 77.7" | 78.0" | 78.0" | 79.3" | 72.2" |
| Tread-front | 58.8" | 59.0" | 59.0" | 60.9" | 57.7" |
| Tread-rear | 58.8" | 56.4" | 56.4" | 59.6" | 58.0" |
| Weight (curb) | 3,602 lbs. | 3,485 lbs. | 3,630 lbs. | 3,440 lbs. | 2,947 lbs. |
| Turning Diameter (wall to wall – max.) | 37.73 ft. | 42.91 ft. | 43.41 ft. | 45.1 ft. | 39.4 ft. |

# 1958 INTERIOR ROOM COMPARISONS OF FOUR-DOOR SEDANS

| | CHEVROLET | FORD CUSTOM 300 | FORD FAIRLANE | PLYMOUTH | RAMBLER 6 |
|---|---|---|---|---|---|
| Front Headroom | 35.0" | 34.8" | 33.9" | 35.7" | 36.0" |
| Rear Headroom | 34.2" | 33.6" | 33.6" | 34.2" | 35.0" |
| Front Legroom | 44.6" | 43.13" | 43.13" | 45.5" | 43.0" |
| Rear Legroom | 42.7" | 42.74" | 40.72" | 41.5" | 40.0" |
| Front Shoulder Room | 56.4" | 57.56" | 57.26" | 60.5" | 57.7" |
| Rear Shoulder Room | 56.2" | 56.96" | 57.0" | 60.4" | 57.6" |
| Front Hip Room | 62.1" | 60.32" | 59.99" | 63.0" | 59.8" |
| Rear Hip Room | 63.1" | 60.32" | 60.12" | 62.7" | 60.1" |

## 1958 CHEVROLET ENGINE CHART

| ENGINE | HP @ RPM | TORQUE @ RPM |
|---|---|---|
| 235.5 c.i.d. Base 6 | 145 @ 4200 | 215 @ 2400 |
| 283 c.i.d. 2-bbl. V-8 | 185 @ 4600 | 275 @ 2400 |
| 283 c.i.d. 4-bbl. V-8 | 230 @ 4800 | 300 @ 3000 |
| 283 c.i.d. Fuel Injection V-8 | 250 @ 5000 | 305 @ 3800 |
| 348 c.i.d. 4-bbl. V-8 | 250 @ 4400 | 355 @ 2800 |
| 348 c.i.d. 3x2-bbl. V-8 | 280 @ 4800 | 355 @ 3200 |

## 1958 CHEVROLET CORVETTE ENGINE CHART

| ENGINE | HP @ RPM | TORQUE @ RPM |
|---|---|---|
| 283 c.i.d. 4-bbl. V-8 | 230 @ 4800 | 300 @ 3000 |
| 283 c.i.d. 2x4-bbl. V-8 | 245 @ 5000 | 300 @ 3800 |
| 283 c.i.d. Fuel Injection V-8 | 250 @ 5000 | 305 @ 3800 |
| 283 c.i.d. 2x4-bbl. V-8* | 270 @ 6000 | 285 @ 4200 |
| 283 c.i.d. Fuel Injection V-8* | 290 @ 6200 | 290 @ 4400 |

* Special Camshaft

## 1958 FORD ENGINE CHART

| ENGINE | HP @ RPM | TORQUE @ RPM |
|---|---|---|
| 223 c.i.d. Base 6 | 145 @ 4200 | 212 @ 2100 |
| 292 c.i.d. 2-bbl. V-8 | 205 @ 4600 | 295 @ 2400 |
| 332 c.i.d. 2-bbl. V-8 | 240 @ 4600 | 340 @ 2400 |
| 332 c.i.d. 4-bbl. V-8 | 265 @ 4600 | 360 @ 2800 |
| 352 c.i.d. 4-bbl. V-8 | 300 @ 4600 | 395 @ 2800 |

## 1958 PLYMOUTH ENGINE CHART

| ENGINE | HP @ RPM | TORQUE @ RPM |
|---|---|---|
| 230 c.i.d. Base 6 | 132 @ 3600 | 205 @ 1200 |
| 318 c.i.d. 4-bbl. V-8 | 250 @ 4400 | 340 @ 2800 |
| 318 c.i.d. 2-bbl. V-8 | 225 @ 4400 | 330 @ 2800 |
| 350 c.i.d. 2x4-bbl. V-8 | 305 @ 5000 | 370 @ 3600 |
| 318 c.i.d. 2x4-bbl. V-8 (Fury) | 290 @ 5200 | 330 @ 3600 |
| 350 c.i.d. Fuel Injection V-8 | 315 @ 5000 | 370 @ 3600 |

## 1958 RAMBLER ENGINE CHART

| ENGINE | HP @ RPM | TORQUE @ RPM |
|---|---|---|
| 195.6 c.i.d. 1-bbl. 6 | 127 @ 4200 | 180 @ 1600 |
| 195.6 c.i.d. 2-bbl. 6 | 138 @ 4500 | 185 @ 1800 |
| 250 c.i.d. 4-bbl. V-8 | 215 @ 4900 | 260 @ 2500 |

# 1958 CHEVROLET
## COLOR CHART

- Snowcrest White
- Aegean Turquoise
- Honey Beige
- Cashmere Blue
- Colonial Cream
- Fathom Blue
- Anniversary Gold
- Cay Coral
- Glen Green
- Rio Red
- Forest Green
- Sierra Gold
- Tropic Turquoise
- Silver Blue
- Onyx Black
- Onyx Black/Arctic White
- Silver Blue/Snowcrest White
- Colonial Cream/Arctic White
- Cay Coral/Arctic White
- Anniversary Gold/Honey Beige
- Rio Red/Arctic White
- Arctic White/Glen Green
- Arctic White/Sierra Gold
- Arctic White/Tropic Turquoise
- Forest Green/Glen Green
- Aegean Turquoise/Arctic White
- Aegean Turquoise/Tropic Turquoise
- Arctic White/Cashmere Blue
- Fathom Blue/Cashmere Blue

# 1958 CHEVROLET
## CORVETTE
## COLOR CHART

### SOLID COLORS

- Signet Red
- Snowcrest White
- Panama Yellow
- Silver Blue
- Regal Turquoise
- Charcoal

### TWO-TONE COLORS

- Signet Red/Snowcrest White
- Snowcrest White/Inca Silver
- Panama Yellow/Snowcrest White
- Silver Blue/Inca Silver
- Regal Turquoise/Snowcrest White
- Charcoal/Inca Silver

## 59

This front view of a 1959 Chevrolet Impala convertible shows the 79.9 inch width and low 54.0 inch height. The model 1867 V-8 had an advertised price of $3,120.75. The Turbo-Thrust engine, indicated by the crossed flags, added $80.70, $172.20, $150.65 or $195.85 depending on specific horsepower rating.

# 1959:
# Cat's Eyes
# and bat wings

There were lessons for Chevrolet in the 1957 sales upset. Foremost of these related to being too conservative for the buyers of the 1950s. These folks wanted their new cars to look new, be trendsetters. The all-new 1958 Chevrolet had been new enough to blow the oddly facelifted 1958 Ford right off the sales charts.

The 1959 follow-up was calculated to be the triumph of the decade. It would be the culmination of all the styling progress of the 1950s, the ultimate in low, wide and bold. It was, in fact, to be so wide that GM had to work with several states to abolish regulations that would have mandated clearance lights on the 1959 Chevrolets. Fins were in and the new Chevrolet would have fins. Not just fins but horizontal fins that would be fresh and unique. All 1959 GM vehicles would depend on fins but, unlike Chrysler

Corporation look-alikes, each division would have their own version. The closest approach to Chevrolet's was that of Buick whose taillights and deck lid were sufficiently different to insure that they would not be confused with each other. Pontiac and Olds were quite different and Cadillac elected to go with huge vertical fins incorporating taillights with long, pointed rocket-like lenses. Some of the GM rooflines, especially on the four-door post sedans and two-door hardtops were rather Chrysler-like but the windshield pillars were totally different. All told, the General Motors family was unique and each division, while sharing the overall concept, was unique unto itself.

The Chevrolet for 1959 was not easy to ignore and not likely to be mistaken for anything else on the road. The horizontal fins reminded many of wings; some said bat wings while others said gull wings. Whatever, they suggested flight and that was good. (Some that drove them claimed that those Chevys actually began to lift a bit when driven at irresponsible speeds. That would not be good, but the author, after 40 plus years, still doesn't believe those claims.) The recessed license plate was hinged to provide access to the fuel filler, which was centered just above the bumper. Huge, horizontal teardrop-shaped taillights were divided by five recessed ribs. These lights quickly earned the nickname "cat's eyes." Optional backup lamps were located in the lower valance panels. Up front, the blade-type bumper was topped by a wide, horizontal grille with nine horizontal bars and seven vertical dividers, each capped off with a bright concave tipped "bullet" which, delighted Chevrolet employees

Model 1839, an Impala Sport Sedan, shows the two-tone paint treatment and new extended roof and deep-curved rear window. The window provided unprecedented rear vision and the extended roof protected rear passengers from too much direct sunlight.

discovered, made a perfect shot glass. The dual headlights were positioned, in a pair of anodized aluminum bezels, at the extreme outboard ends of the grille. The parking/turn signal lights were situated within the tips of two slender air inlets at the lower edge of the hood. These inlets were separated by a body-color section of hood, which hosted a "Chevrolet" script nameplate and, on V-8 models, a broad V. The front license plate was centered under the grille with a body color valance panel on either side. The side view was totally contemporary with the top surface of the fin extending nearly half of the vehicle's length forming a ledge over a deeply sculpted body line that swept back and around to form the upper surface of the taillight housing. The front fender was also deeply sculptured with a high, horizontal character line. The wrap-around windshield flowed into a low, flat roof.

Chevrolet, having received completely new chassis in 1955 and again in 1958, was significantly improved again in 1959. The official word as printed in the 1959 dealer album tended to exaggerate a bit: "It's all new all over again and significantly different from the road up!" In reality, an analysis of the components suggests "extensively tweaked" would be a more accurate description than "all new." The front suspension, for example, received stronger mountings. The Impala, station wagons, and all V-8 models featured a standard front stabilizer bar. In the four-link rear suspension, new lower control arm mounting, larger control arm bushings, new upper control arm and a new lateral stabilizer contributed to increased "road sense" and improved isolation from shock and

vibration. In effect, this was an improved version of the excellent full coil suspension, introduced in 1958, which brought a coil spring to each wheel. Level Air Ride was available, at extra cost, for the second and last time. Chevrolet described it as "a ride second to none – it's true more than ever with 1959 Level Air. It's the simplest, most trouble-free design in the industry, now offering an even more luxurious ride." In the Level Air system, each of the four coil springs was replaced by an air bag, which was supplied by an engine-mounted compressor.

The X-shaped frame, which eliminated side rails, was continued for 1959. This frame contributed to the low overall height. The design relied on beefed-up body side rails (rocker panels) which provided rigidity and side impact resistance. Brakes boasted 27 percent more lining area with improved flow of air for better cooling. These Safety-Master brakes were said to be 66 percent more durable.

The base engine was the familiar 235-cubic-inch Hi-Thrift 6, now rated at 135 hp, down from 145 hp in 1958. A contemporary publication said that this was the result of fine-tuning to increase economy in response to the public revolt against wasteful cars. Chevrolet more or less confirmed this with this blurb in the 1959 dealer album. "New economy-contoured camshaft and modified valve lifters are responsible for the 6's new performance. Valves remain closed longer, producing higher engine efficiency at lower, more usable speeds. The Hi-Thrift 6 featured full-pressure lubrication, full-length water jackets and hydraulic valve lifters.

Chevrolet's least expensive four-door sedan was this 1959 Biscayne six-cylinder model 1119. In this totally base condition it weighed 3,605 pounds and had an advertised price of $2,301.

The highly regarded 283 was back with the 185-horse, two-barrel, Turbo-Fire V-8. The torque rating was 275 at 2,400 rpm. New features included a dry air cleaner and a new integral fuel filter. Dual exhaust was optional.

The 283 Super Turbo-Fire V-8 added a four-barrel carburetor and 9.5:1 compression for 230 hp at 4,800 rpm. Torque was 300 at 3,000 rpm. Single exhaust was standard and dual exhaust was optional.

Once again the 283 was the basis for the Ramjet Fuel Injection V-8 which developed its 250 horsepower at 5,000 rpm with torque rated at 305 at 3,800. Hydraulic lifters and dual exhaust were employed. In a rather strange move Chevrolet decided to make this performance engine look a bit friendlier by revealing that "overall economy is excellent."

If the 250-horsepower 283 was a bit below buyer expectations, the Ramjet Special Fuel Injection V-8 with 10.5:1 compression, special camshaft and valve system with low-weight valves and mechanical valve lifters, premium-quality bearings and other special components engineered for extreme operating conditions might be just the ticket. Horsepower was kicked up to 290 at 6,200 rpm and torque was 290 at 4,400 rpm.

The 348, introduced in 1958, was back in spades. The entry level 348 was the four-barrel Turbo-Thrust which made 250 hp at 4,400 rpm with torque rated at 355 at 2,800 rpm. Compression was 9.5:1 and dual exhaust was standard.

The Turbo-Thrust Special V-8 featured an ultra-high compression ratio of 11:1 to develop 305 hp at 5,600 rpm. Torque was rated at 350 at 3,600 rpm.

The Super Turbo-Thrust V-8 was yet another 9.5:1 compression 348, this time with hydraulic valve lifters and triple two-barrel carburetion developing 280 hp at 4,800 rpm with a torque reading of 355 at 3,200 rpm.

Capping off the engine lineup for 1959 was the Super Turbo-Thrust Special V-8 with special camshaft and valve system with mechanical lifters, ultra-high compression ratio of 11:1 and extra heavy duty components throughout. The pre-announcement advertised horsepower of 315 was raised to 335 at 5,800 rpm with torque rated at 362 at 3,600 rpm.

Over forty years later, as this is being written, in an age of minimal plant complexity and de-proliferation, it seems like corporate madness that this engine lineup could have existed. The somewhat unpredictable and very expensive fuel injection was now a Chevrolet exclusive and lived right alongside more powerful, more reliable, less expensive 348 Super Turbo-Thrust V-8s. In commenting on this situation on October 27, 1958, Arthur Railton, automotive editor of *Popular Mechanics*, speculated that Fuel Injection existed at Chevrolet only because Ed Cole, Chevrolet's general manager, was a determined engineer who would not "admit that he can't build a dependable, reliable injection system at a reasonable cost and he'll do it one of these years."

Look carefully. This is a proposed 1959 Bel Air Sport Coupe, a model that was never produced. It is probably a full size fiberglass model. Those wheel covers didn't make it. The centered backup light was rejected in favor of twin units.

Chevrolet passenger cars were marketed in five series in 1959. The Impala was at the top of the line. The Bel Air was somewhat de-contented and demoted to the mid-level position previously occupied by the Biscayne. The Biscayne, in turn, was bumped down to the level of the previous entry level Delray to compete for the no frills crowd. The Delray was discontinued. Station wagons continued to be treated as a separate series with models corresponding to Impala, Bel Air and Biscayne trim levels. Rounding out the line, of course, was the prestigious Corvette sports car.

The Impala, which had been two models in the Bel Air line in 1958, was now a complete line including a four-door sedan, Sport Sedan (four-door flat-top hardtop), Sport Coupe (two-door hardtop), and convertible. The Sport Sedan was the style leader, with the flat top roof design used by all GM divisions. Chevrolet described it like this: "A beautiful new model in a brand-new series. The striking extended roof and deep-curved rear window add unmistakable smartness and wide-range rear vision." This was more than a styling gimmick. In many contemporary vehicles, including the Sport Coupe, the sharply angled back window extended above the heads of the rear seat passengers who could become very uncomfortable on a sunny day. The extended roof of the Sport Sedan effectively protected the rear seat passengers from the unpleasant sensation of unwanted sunstroke. Rear vision was about as close to unobstructed as possible. The regular four-door, six-window sedan, while not as likely as the Sport Coupe to bake the guys in the back, featured a stylish, sloping roofline. Speaking of the

glass area on the Sport Coupe, Chevrolet claimed that "total visibility area is almost 50 percent greater." All 1959 Chevrolets offered a wrap-over, wraparound "Vista-Panoramic" windshield.

The interior of the 1959 Impala was nothing short of wild. Over the past few years, the emphasis had shifted from luxury to bold displays of color. The soft broadcloths and velours of a few years ago were nowhere to be found in most carlines. Impala four-door sedans were available in five colors; light and medium gray, light and medium yellow-green, light and medium blue, light and medium copper, and light and medium turquoise. All other Impala body styles featured those colors as well as red. Impala interiors were largely vinyl with seating surfaces of nylon-faced tri-colored pattern cloth. Front and rear cushions were foam rubber padded. Full carpeting was standard on closed models while convertibles featured carpet-textured vinyl-coated floor mats. The backrests of convertibles and Sport Coupes were notched to accommodate a recessed grille for the optional rear seat speaker. The interior of the four-door sedan differed from that of the other Impalas in several respects. The post sedan incorporated conventional armrests while the other Impala models sported long armrests with built-in safety reflectors and fingertip door handles on more dramatic door panels. Post sedans also lacked the wide, bright metal front seat end panels found on the other Impalas. Hardtops had embossed vinyl headlining while those in post sedans were stitched-up using textured cloth. Impala instrument panels featured a large round speedometer with an electric clock and a

Chevrolet's fanciest 1959 Wagon was this Nomad, a six-passenger, four-door sharing the Impala trim level. An eight-cylinder model 1835, it carried an advertised price of $3,009. The full wheel covers added $24 and the 8.00 x 14 whitewalls another $35.85.

parking brake-warning light joining the instruments in four-hooded circular pods. The lower half was dressed up with a wall-to-wall bright textured applique. According to the Chevrolet dealer album, "The distinctive sports-car-inspired steering wheel features a new clear-view horn ring." This attractive wheel was usually finished in two-tones, the exception being the single color red steering wheel which was supplied with the red interior. The red interior, not used with post sedans, was the only one in which the vinyl was not two-toned using light and medium shades.

The interior of the Bel Air, while not Spartan, was a definite cut below those established in previous years. The instrument panel now had a thin, mid-level wall-to-wall bright molding, lacking the wide, bright, textured applique of the Impala. The steering wheel was a simple, single tone affair with a half-circle horn ring. The clock became an option but cigarette lighter, glove compartment lock and light and automatic interior light switches were still standard. Foam rubber front seat cushion was standard and twin visors were provided. Armrests, front and rear, were, of course, provided and those in the rear carried ashtrays.

Bel Air interiors were available in five colors; light and medium gray, light and medium yellow-green, light and medium blue, light and medium copper and light and medium turquoise. Door trim panels were trimmed in two shades of vinyl. Seating surfaces were upholstered in a geometric pattern cloth trimmed in medium tone leather-grain vinyl. Light-tone textured cloth headlining was color-keyed. The color-keyed floor

covering was an attractive combination of carpet and vinyl-rubber with the carpet used on the tunnel area and rubber-vinyl covering the high wear surfaces.

The Biscayne interior was predictably low in luxury content but at least there was some color choice with the two-door sedan and the four-door sedan. Light and medium gray, light and medium yellow-green and light and medium blue interiors were completely color keyed. If the buyer selected the Biscayne utility sedan the interior color choice was simple; light and medium gray ... period. The steering wheel employed a central horn button; no horn ring was available. The instrument panel trim molding used on the Bel Air was deleted. When not hosting the optional radio and its bright bezel, this was one plain instrument panel.

Door trim panels and sidewalls featured a soft-rolled upper edge, which looked more costly while eliminating separate garnish moldings. These panels were two-toned and featured embossed patterns. Seating surfaces featured spatter pattern cloth while bolsters were trimmed in embossed, light tone leather-grain vinyl. The rubber floor mats were coated with color-keyed vinyl for easy maintenance. The headliner was cut from light-tone textured cloth. While front and rear armrests and right hand sun visor were not on the standard features list, they could be purchased with cigarette lighter and front fender ornaments in option package RPO 347. The utility sedan offered a huge in-car cargo area with the entire rear passenger compartment covered by a rubber carpeted flat platform. The sidewalls were done in two toned

A family favorite, the 1959 Bel Air four-door sedan, model 1519 (6) or 1619 (V-8) is shown with two-tone paint, a $26.90 option, and 7.50 x 14 whitewalls which listed at $31.55.

leather-grain vinyl. A painted fiber board back wall sealed off the trunk area. Rear windows were fixed in the up position.

Impala exteriors were even beyond the expectations of many new car buyers in 1959. In a move away from the exotic trim applications of most makes in previous years, the Impala side trim treatment was less complicated. The body side molding was wide and ran the full length of the body. The rear half of this molding featured a colored insert area with an Impala nameplate and emblem. The top of each front fender carried a rocket-inspired ornament with a bright molding trailing back to the door cut. The rear deck outline (fin edge) carried a bright molding that began on the back door of four-door models (or just behind the front door on two-door models) and outlined the overhanging fin, swept into the decklid and continued around to the fin's leading edge on the other side. A separate molding was applied at the center of the decklid. Other bright moldings outlined the license plate recess and surrounded all window areas. Sport sedans and sport coupes had an extra-wide roof side molding. All closed models now had the simulated roof vent introduced on the 1958 Impala Sport Coupe. Standard back-up lamps were located below the rear bumper.

Bel Air exteriors were somewhat de-contented but still attractive. While maintaining the rocket-inspired front fender ornaments, the Bel Air did not get the fender crown moldings that went almost to the windshield of Impalas. The Bel Air body side molding ran the entire length of the vehicle and featured an ivory (white) painted center. The roof side moldings of the Impala were replaced by thin bright drip rail moldings, no window reveal moldings were employed and the deck lid center molding, side window surrounds, deck lid center molding and license plate recess moldings were omitted. Gone also were the stripes on the taillights and that neat Impala simulated roof vent. The bright moldings edging the rear deck and fin edges were maintained, as were windshield and backlight reveal moldings.

In its day, and when compared to the Impala, the Biscayne was not a highly trimmed vehicle. However, judged by the less glitzy standards of a different millennium, the vehicle was quite attractive. The major difference between Bel Air and Biscayne exteriors was in the Biscayne's elimination of the roof drip rail moldings, front fender ornaments and full-length body side moldings. Those moldings were replaced by a thinner molding on front fenders and front doors. The deck lid and fin edge moldings were retained as were windshield and backlight reveal moldings. When equipped with a few options, such as whitewalls, wheel covers and rear antenna, for example, the Biscayne was a pretty well turned out car.

In 1959 the American family was enjoying a long-term love affair with the station wagon and Chevrolet had quite a line of wagons. At the top, the Nomad was a gleaming beauty employing the Impala-level trim. The Nomad was available in six-passenger capacity only. The second seat was re-engineered to

**'59**

The simulated air exhaust can be seen centered on the roof of this 1959 Impala four-door sedan. The backup lights, standard on Impala, are under the bumper. The full wheel covers are a $24 accessory. The 7:50 x 14 whitewalls added $31.55 to the advertised price of a $2,710 V-8 model 1819.

fold flat with minimum effort, the cushion remaining in place with the backrest folding over it. The load floor utilized a vinyl-coated covering that resembled linoleum. Interior fabrics and materials were those used in the Impala with the exception of the embossed vinyl headlining.

The Parkwood and Kingswood wagons shared the interior and exterior features characteristic of the Bel Air trim level. The Parkwood was a six-passenger, two-seat model. The Kingswood was Chevrolet's only nine-passenger, three-seat model. This year the third seat was a real seat and it faced rearward. Like the Plymouth of last year, the window lowered into the tailgate and the tailgate could then be folded down. The window was power operated on Kingswood models, manual on six-passenger models. The power tailgate window was an available option for Nomad and Parkwood models. This window in power or manual versions became a problem when the vehicles aged and the mechanism rusted, preventing use of the tailgate. When power equipped, the window could be operated by key at the tailgate or from inside by switches near the third seat or on the firewall. At entry level, comparable to the Biscayne sedans, were the Brookwood wagons in two-door and four-door versions. Both were six-passenger, two-seat models. This was, of course, Chevrolet's sole remaining two-door wagon. These wagons enjoyed success in fleet applications. The two-door Brookwood was also popular with parents of young children who feared accidental opening of rear doors.

The Corvette had been given a massive facelift in 1958 and 1959 was a year of sophistication for that facelift. There were two very noticeable styling refinements; the removal of the chrome "suspenders" on the rear deck and the elimination of the simulated hood louvers. Wheel covers were slightly modified with a series of slots added to the outer edge. Interior modifications were minor. Five Corvette engines were available in 1959, all based on the 283 cid small block. The base engine was a four-barrel with 9.5:1 compression ratio and hydraulic lifters developing 230 horses at 4,800 rpm and 300 lbs./ft. of torque at 3,000 rpm. A twin four-barrel version with 9.5:1 compression ratio and hydraulic lifters made 245 horses at 5,000 rpm and 300 lbs./ft. of torque at 3,800 rpm. The lowest rated fuel injection powerplant was a 9.5:1 compression ratio version using hydraulic lifters. It made 250 horsepower at 5,000 rpm and 305 lbs./ft. of torque at 3,800 rpm. The twin four-barrel 283, when equipped with special camshaft with high rpm valve system with special valves and mechanical valve lifters made 270 horses at 6,000 rpm. Torque dropped to 285 lbs./ft. at 4,200 rpm. The top producer was the 10.5:1 compression ratio fuel-injected 283-cid V-8 with special camshaft with high rpm valve system and mechanical valve lifters. It was rated at 290 hp at 6,200 rpm. The base transmission was a close-ratio three-speed manual. The first option was the four-speed close-ratio Synchro-Mesh. Powerglide was available with the 230-hp, 245-hp and 250-hp engines.

GM had set out to prove that they could conceive and develop the most dramatic and impressive automobiles in North America. In that, the corporation

The Parkwood, a four-door, six-passenger station wagon, shared the Bel Air's interior and exterior trim. This Parkwood is shown with 8:00 x 14 whitewalls, a $35.85 option and two-tone paint that added $32.30 to the price of a V-8 model 1635, which had an advertised price of $2,867.

definitely accomplished what it set out to do in creating these huge land yachts. The question is "did they go too far?" It appears that they did just that. While many people were simply bowled over by these new Chevys, there were a growing number of buyers who were uncomfortable with the sheer bulk. They had a mentor, American Motors President, George Romney, who had found a niche for his line of compact, conservative Ramblers. Under Romney AMC advertising harpooned the "gigantic dinosaurs" that his major domestic competitors were offering. Cartoon ads in the major magazines ridiculed the big-finned cars. One of the more memorable of these ads depicted a dinghy slung between the towering fins of one of these large vehicles. Nash and Hudson, the forerunners of AMC, had been pioneers in unitized construction and the Ramblers enjoyed the added space efficiency and strength that could result from this construction. While considerably smaller than the traditional "low-priced-three," the bolt upright Ramblers offered six-passenger seating and adequate luggage capacity.

The overhead valve 195-cid six-cylinder engine was a modern design that developed 127 horses, adequate for many thrift-minded Americans. A two-barrel version raised that horsepower to 138. For the Ramblerite who needed V-8 power, the 250 cid four-barrel developing 215 horses was available but not very popular as most buyers felt that the six did the job. The Rambler was about 20 inches shorter overall, 2 inches taller, and 7.5 inches narrower than the Biscayne and weighed 669 pounds less. Inside, the Biscayne led the

Rambler in seven out of eight interior measurements. Again, the Rambler had the same passenger capacity – 6, so no big deal to some folks. The re-born Rambler American of 1958 was back, this time with a cute little two-door wagon resurrected form 1950-55 production.

Studebaker had been on a skid for some time now. The sedans and wagons of 1953 had been facelifted to the point that they were on the verge of weird. There wasn't much development money lying around and Studebaker really needed some new product. At times like that, companies sometimes get unexpectedly creative and Studebaker spent a few dollars and got very creative. Using mostly existing components, Studebaker designers and engineers cut the wheelbase to 108 inches with overhang cut to just 26.4 inches in front and 40.06 inches out back. That compares to Biscayne's wheelbase of 119.0 inches, front and rear overhang of 32.6 inches and 59.3 inches, respectively. Studebaker didn't have Chevrolet's roomy interior but six-passengers could be accommodated. The new Lark, as it was called, had a rather anemic base six-cylinder engine that made just 90 horses at 4,000 rpm. The 259.2-cid V-8 came in two flavors; 180 horse two-barrel and 195 horse four-barrel. The Lark was offered in two-door sedan, four-door sedan, two-door hardtop and two-door wagon body styles. The Lark, by Studebaker standards, was a huge success. Percentage of the industry doubled over 1958 from 1.18 percent to 2.36 percent for 1959. By the way, the wheezy little 169.6 cid flathead six far outsold the V-8s. That fact alone shows the mood of the 1959 car buyer.

The lowest price four-door station wagon was this Brookwood six-passenger which utilized Biscayne level interior and exterior trim. This model 1235 V-8 had an advertised price of $2,756. The 8:00 x 14 whitewall tires added $35.85.

The imports were multiplying like cockroaches in 1959. The winner was, of course, VW but the handsome and problem prone Renault Dauphine, a water-cooled rear engine four-door, actually outsold VW in some reporting periods during 1959. The sporty Renault Caravelle was brought in to fight VW's sleek Karmann-Ghia. VW's design origin was obviously rooted in the 1930s and the American public, while craving handling ease and operating economy, was still impressed by nice lines. For that reason, and scarcity of new VW's at the dealerships, Renault Dauphines sold in vast numbers to Americans, many of whom, especially in the salt belt, would wish that they had waited for a VW.

The Big Three domestic manufacturers packed some of their European built small cars on boats and let their dealers get somewhat involved in the import business. Ford had been selling fairly decent British-built cars in the U.S. and Canada (especially Canada) since the end of WWII. The most popular of these in 1959 were the Anglia and Prefect, tiny four-cylinder models on a 90.5-inch wheelbase. They were popular enough to grab third place in import sales in 1959.

Buick and Pontiac dealers were selling imports in 1959. Buick had the Opel Rekord, a very pretty little German car in two-door sedan or two-door wagon body styles. The very conventional Rekord had a water-cooled front-mounted 57-horsepower engine driving the rear wheels through a three-speed manual transmission. Opel was fourth in import sales in the U.S. in 1959. Pontiac dealers handled the Vauxhall from England. It too was a well-dressed little car with totally conventional layout. It was available as either a four-door sedan or four-door wagon. It was not as well received as the Opel.

Chrysler went shopping for a European affiliate in the mid-1950s and wound up buying Simca of France from Ford. Simca dealers had a full line of cars to sell ranging from a little two-passenger convertible that showed its previous kinship to the '55 T-Bird, through a series of four-cylinder sedans, two-door hardtops, and wagons, to a couple of V-8 sedans. Not just V-8 but flathead V-8. Remember the V-8 60? Well, that wound up in France and by 1959, with 84 horses now, was powering a slick 106-inch wheelbase sedan. Like many French cars, the Simca proved to be too quirky for most Americans but it was an interesting effort.

Ford continued to be the direct competition. Reversing the pattern set in 1957 and 1958, all Fords used the same 118-inch wheelbase, one inch shorter than the new Chevrolet. Overall, the Ford was two inches shorter. Both cars were virtually the same height and width. The Chevrolet (Biscayne four-door vs. Custom 300 four-door) out-weighed Ford by almost 400 pounds. The Chevrolet also beat the Ford in front and rear headroom, front and rear leg room, front and rear shoulder room and front and rear hip room. While the 1957 Fords had been a styling success, the 1958 models were not generally considered to be a successful facelift. The 1959 Fords were, at the time, viewed as both conservative and attractive. A wide, forward thrusting grille and well-integrated quad headlamps

The 235-cid six-cylinder engine, renamed Hi-Thrift 6, was claimed to deliver as much as 10 percent greater fuel economy with more torque thanks to a new economy camshaft.

characterized the front. In profile the impression was one of a large and dignified vehicle.

From the rear, Fords again looked like Fords with large round taillights replacing the unpopular quad ovals of 1958. At introduction time Fords were offered in Custom 300, Fairlane and Fairlane 500 series. Shortly after announcement, the Galaxie series was added at the top of the line. Actually, the Fairlane 500 and the Galaxie were identical except for the badging and the shape of the rear pillar and backlight. The Fairlane 500 closed models featured a wraparound backlight while the Galaxie picked up the Thunderbird treatment with a wide rear pillar and a nearly flat recessed backlight. With Galaxie production at about 465,000 and Fairlane 500 production in the range of 80,000, it appears that the Fairlane 500 series was phased out shortly after the Galaxie was phased in. The Galaxie, while boxy, was certainly not lacking for bright trim. In fact a comparison between the Impala and the Galaxie reveals that there is much more glittery trim hung on the Ford than there is on the Chevrolet. Chevrolet, with deeply drawn metal and flowing lines, didn't need much trim. Ford did need that trim because some of it was used to actually change the vehicle's lines.

Galaxie interiors featured the nicest instrument panel to grace a Ford in a few years. The instruments and controls were grouped in front of the driver behind a characteristic Ford deep-dish steering wheel. Interior fabrics were colorful, employing pleated cloth, metallic-tint vinyls, Mylar and white vinyl accents. Mid-level

Fairlanes, lacking some of the Galaxie's eye diverting trim, took on a chunkier, high-belted look. The Fairlane was also deprived of the Galaxie's Thunderbird-inspired rear roof pillar, a mixed blessing. While the wider roof pillar was a successful styling cue, the wraparound backlight certainly improved vision to the right rear corner. Unlike Chevrolet's Bel Air line, which included a four-door hardtop, Ford no longer offered hardtops in the mid-priced line. If the buyer wanted a hardtop, it was necessary to kick in the extra cash to move up to the Galaxie. The Custom 300 offered four-door sedans, two-door sedans, and business coupe (six-cylinder only) models. Once again, some trim, interior and exterior, was deleted. The Custom 300 models looked very high belted from the side, rather tall from the rear. Further evidence of the mood of the 1959 buyer is found in the fact that Ford's two best sellers, by a long shot, were the Custom 300 four-door sedan and two-door sedan, in that order.

Ford's engine lineup for 1959 was very limited compared to Chevrolet's selection of 10 engines. Ford elected to let just four engines do the job. It is interesting to note that each engine displacement was available in just one configuration and that only one engine featured a four-barrel carburetor. No tri-powers, no dual-quads, not much of anything except economy. The entry level one-barrel 223 in-line six made 145 horses at 4,000 rpm and 206 lbs./ft. of torque at 2,200 rpm. The base V-8 was the two-barrel 292, which developed 200 horses at 4,400 rpm and 285 lbs./ft. of torque at 2,200 rpm. The first optional V-8 was the two-barrel 332, which was rated at 225 horses at

Perhaps the young lady is resting her feet at an auto show. More likely, she is showing us that we can sit on the trunk of a 1959 Corvette without getting ridges on our backsides from the twin bars that graced the trunk of the 1958 Corvette.

4,400 rpm. The torque rating was 325 lbs./ft. at 2,200 rpm. The largest available engine and the only one available with a four-barrel which made 300 horses at 2,800 rpm and 380 lbs./ft. of torque at 2,800 rpm. Chevrolet, of course, had three engines with horsepower ratings exceeding Ford's best.

Station wagons had always been a bright spot for Ford and 1959 was no exception as Ford again outsold Chevrolet in wagons. This may have been a chore for Ford salesmen as their wagon was a bit archaic in several areas. The first relates to the tailgate design in which the window was located in the upper portion of a two-piece tailgate. Chevrolet's new gate design offered the convenience of being able to lower the window into the gate from the driver's seat, allowing someone at the rear of the vehicle to empty the grocery cart or load lumber or whatever. Ford's configuration required that the person in the rear have a key or that the driver leave the warm confines of the front seat to open the tailgate. Another Chevrolet feature, the third facing rear seat, used a real seat with real cushions that didn't have to be removed and stashed someplace to get a flat cargo floor. Ford offered six wagon models, two were two-doors, and four were four-doors. At the bottom of the line were the two-door and four-door six-passenger Ranch Wagons. The popular four-door, six or nine-passenger Country Sedans were joined by a two-door model. The two-door Country Sedan was available only in six-passenger form. The top-of-the-line offering continued to be the woodgrained Country Squire, available only as a nine-passenger model. The best seller was the six-passenger Country Sedan.

Plymouth, which had been in automotive purgatory in 1958 for the high crimes of 1957, was trying to get some credibility back in 1959. Plymouth had introduced a very advanced chassis in 1957 incorporating longitudinal torsion bar front suspension. The ride was good, the handling and road holding superb, but reliability was terrible. The same could be said for the optional three-speed Torqueflite automatic transmission, and most of the engines. The stylish bodies leaked and/or fell apart and even the upholstery was of shoddy quality. Now, in 1959, those bodies were in their third year and on their second facelift. While still sleeker and more modern looking than the 1959 Fords, the Plymouth was now competing against a very new, very low, very long looking Chevrolet. And remember Chevrolet's quality reputation, based on the 1957 models, was pretty good. In terms of size the Plymouth was less than an inch shorter than the Chevy. The Chevy was almost two inches wider and the Plymouth 0.6 inches taller. Plymouth had a slightly wider front and rear tread. Using base four-door sedans for comparison, Chevrolet outweighed Plymouth by 330 pounds but had a turning circle 1.5 feet tighter. Of the eight standard interior dimensions, Chevrolet led Plymouth in five, tied in one.

Plymouth entered 1959 with an expanded model lineup; 29 models, to be exact. The truly unique Fury of 1956-58 was gone. The new top-of-the-line was the less unique, less pricey Sport Fury, now offered in two-door hardtop and convertible models. The Fury line consisted of two-door and four-door hardtops and a four-door sedan. The former top dog, the Belvedere,

## 59

This 1959 Impala Convertible was shot in one of Chevrolet's engineering shops. The transmission selector is for a Turboglide model; Turboglide was priced at $242. The power windows added $102.25; deluxe heater, $80.25; and Wonderbar radio, $121.50. A 1959 Corvette can be seen through the windshield.

was offered in two-door and four-door sedans and hardtops and a convertible. The Savoy was now the entry-level series in two-door and four-door sedans and a business coupe. Three four-door station wagons and two two-door wagons rounded out the line.

Like Ford, Plymouth offered four engines. The entry-level one-barrel, 230-cid L-head six was now making its final appearance. With a great deal of straining, the old boat-anchor managed 132 horses at 3,600 rpm and 205 lbs./ft. of torque at 1,200 rpm. It was short of both Ford (145 hp) and Chevy (135 hp). The base V-8 was the two-barrel 318, which made 230 horses at 4,400 rpm and 340 lbs./ft. of torque at 2,400 rpm. That same 318 with four-barrel was good for 260 horses at 4,400 rpm and 345 lbs./ft. of torque at 2,800 rpm. This was the standard engine with the Sport Fury. At the top of Plymouth's line was the four-barrel 361 V-8 developing 305 horses at 4,600 rpm with 395 lbs./ft. of torque. Now listen closely and you'll learn about a neat little trick used by Plymouth, Buick and maybe others. Plymouth merchandised that 361 V-8 as the "Golden Commando 395 Engine." Did you catch it? You were supposed to think that the "395" part referred to horsepower, or maybe even cubic inches. But no, "395" was the torque figure. Buick was known for that nonsense, too. Boo! Hiss! for the ad guys! Deception aside, this was a pretty decent little group of engines, with Plymouth stomping both Chevrolet and Ford in entry level and first option V-8s, and Ford on biggest available V-8 as well. Now you know why that kid in study hall kept wiping out the family Impala with his mother's Savoy sedan.

It had been a confusing year for Detroit. When they were designing and tooling up for the 1959 model cars, the public couldn't get enough of longer, lower, wider. Heavy was good and the more power the better. Yes, the increasing interest in VW was noted and the big three thought they were well positioned to combat the import boom with imports of their own. Good idea but not very effective because the products were not the right ones and the public was not real happy with their dealers, the same ones who had stonewalled on the issue of repairing quality problems. AMC, which had dumped the huge Nash and badge-engineered Hudsons at the end of 1957, was looking very sincere in 1959 and worked at capacity to fill the demand for sensible cars. Studebaker, as noted earlier, had hit a home run with the Lark and doubled market share.

Chevrolet, traditionally number one in sales, lost a close one to Ford in 1957. In 1958 Chevrolet's all new car easily outsold Ford's face-lifted model (less T-Bird) by more than 266,000 vehicles. In 1959, with both having new models, the regular Chevrolet outsold the regular Ford by a little over 42,000. Considering the huge volume involved and Chevrolet's tremendous margin of success in 1958, it would appear that the public liked the Ford approach to styling in 1959. Plymouth actually built a better car in 1959, not a perfect car but at least enough better to move public sentiment a bit. Model year sales were under one-half million but Plymouth still managed to hang on to third place in sales. Yes, it was another year of Chevrolet leadership but not really a great one.

Chevrolet's lowest priced six-passenger car was this Biscayne two-door sedan. The Biscayne was downgraded from its mid-level position of 1958 to the entry-level series of 1959, replacing the Delray.

Brand new for 1959, this El Camino may have been a bit light on practicality but it was tops in appearance. It is shown with Bel Air level side moldings, fender ornament (rockets), and whitewalls.

This is Chevrolet's only nine-passenger 1959 station wagon. The small steps, visible on the rear bumper, identified nine-passenger models in which the passengers entered through the tailgate opening and faced rearward. Sharing the Bel Air trim level, a V-8 Kingswood model 1645 had an advertised price of $2,970. The 8:00 x 14 whitewalls were priced at $35.85.

The 1959 Biscayne had a no-frills front passenger compartment. Armrests were an option, which was not ordered for this vehicle. It is a stick shift with a non-glare rear view mirror priced at $5.85; body mount rear view mirror, $5.95; heater, $80; and a manual radio, $63.75.

This 1959 Impala Convertible was one of very few equipped with the $134.50 Level Air Suspension option. The Impala taillight lens was divided by four bright bars. This treatment was exclusive to Impala. Those backup lights were standard for Impala, an $11.45 accessory for all others.

No, it's not just another 1959 Nomad. It's a full-size fiberglass model and, on this side it's a four-door hardtop wagon. This is one that was never produced. Nice, though!

This two-door sedan displays some Bel Air standard features, including the full length body side molding with ivory stripe, bright roof drip rail moldings and front fender ornaments. The whitewalls added $31.55 to the advertised price of $2,386 (6) or $2,504 (V-8).

The beautiful Impala Sport Coupe, a model 1837, is shown with optional two-tone paint, wheel covers and whitewalls. On a 119-inch wheelbase and standing just 54 inches high, this model weighed 3,580 pounds and rode on 7.50 x 14 tires.

Here's one of Chevy's most expensive options for 1959, factory installed air conditioning, which retailed for $468.

This is the passenger compartment of a three-speed 1959 Corvette. An open storage area was now incorporated under the assist bar and seats were modified for improved lateral support.

X29000-637

This prototype 1959 sport coupe was used to try out the accessory continental tire and rear-mount antenna. The antenna was eventually priced at $10.85. The continental kit listed for $216.

A 283 V-8 model 1619 Bel Air four-door sedan is shown with optional two-tone paint, a $26.90 bargain, and 7:50 x 14 whitewalls, which cost $31.55. The two-tone treatment on sedan models covered the roof and the entire rear deck and fin tops. Chevrolet referred to this area as "tailplanes".

In July of 1957, Chevrolet was serious enough about this 1959 proposal that it got to the clay stage. Can you say Edsel?

Top down, boot on and ready for action, the 1959 Chevrolet Impala Convertible shows wide, full-length body side molding with "Impala" letters and emblem. This angle shows the wraparound on the compound-complex windshield. The wheel covers and whitewalls were extra cost.

Shown with the top up and windows down, this 1959 Impala convertible looks odd with its base hubcaps and optional $35.85 whitewalls. The $2,967 car would have benefited from a $24 set of wheelcovers.

In profile, it can be seen that GM's 1959 styling owed a bit to the 1957 Chrysler products. This Impala is distinguished by the bright moldings, which ran above the side windows, and the wide, full-length side molding with color fill on the quarter panel and half of the rear door housing the Impala name. The wheel covers and white walls were extra cost.

This Impala test car is now sporting a floor shift lever. The original column shift collar is still in place. This vehicle has a few accessories and options, including the non-glare mirror, $5.85; Autronic Eye, $57.25; pushbutton radio, $84; heater, $80.25; and body mount rear-view mirror, $5.95.

Chevrolet's least expensive station wagon for 1959 was this two-door Brookwood six-passenger model based on the Biscayne trim level. The six-cylinder model 1115 was priced at $2,571. This V-8 model 1215 had a base price of $2,689.

**'59**

The rear passenger compartment of a Bel Air four-door sedan shows the mix of deep-pile rayon carpet and colored vinyl coated rubber mat used on the floors. The tunnel is carpeted. The ashtray was removed from the seat back and a smaller tray was incorporated in each armrest. Note the embossed V and crossed flags on upper door trim panels. The fabric was metallic geometric design pattern cloth.

This shot of the 1959 Boston Motorama was taken in November of 1958. The cutaway was based on a 1959 Impala Sport Sedan. The car facing the camera is another Impala Sport Sedan. In 1959 that black Impala four-door sedan was rather unusual. The wagon is a nine-passenger Kingswood.

'59

This view of a 1959 Impala Sport Coupe reveals the simulated air exhaust over the rear window and the two-tone paint treatment on the roof and deck area. The paint fill on the quarter panel matched the top color.

The optional, and functional, right rear antenna is listed at $10.85. It is shown on this beautiful white 1959 Impala convertible that also features optional full wheel covers and whitewalls. It's a 348 car as indicated by the crossed flags above the hood V.

This crank down rear window was a new feature for 1959 on all Chevrolet six-passenger station wagons. An electric-operated window was standard on nine-passenger models, optional at $32.30 on six-passenger models. The four bright bars on the taillights identify this as a Nomad.

The 1959 Chevrolet El Camino was a response to Ford's 1957 and 1958 Ranchero. Both had roots in Australia's Utes. This beautiful El Camino was shot at the 1959 Boston Motorama wearing the Bel Air molding treatment, whitewalls and wheel covers. The hood V without crossed flags reveals that this unit was powered by a 283 V-8.

MADLER
7-17-59

16 562

This shot from July of 1957 shows a rear end treatment that is reminiscent of the 1959 Edsel. The side treatment is also best forgotten.

The 1959 Chevrolet Impala four-door sedan was trimmed in the best of 1959 fashion. The seat inserts were nylon-faced tri-colored pattern cloth with bolsters of light-tone leather-grain vinyl. Medium-tone leather-grain vinyl covered the tops of the backrests. Deep pile carpeting was used. "B" posts were vinyl covered. Door accents were in herringbone pattern vinyl.

This angle of the 1959 Impala Sport Sedan shows the immense expanse of glass that swept from rear door opening to rear door opening. The extended roof effectively protected rear passengers from direct contact with the sun's rays. The Impala Sport Sedan, like all closed Impalas, featured a simulated air exhaust at the roof's edge. This vehicle has optional wheel covers, whitewalls and two-tone paint.

This yawning cavity is the cargo area of a 1959 Chevrolet Nomad wagon with the second seat folded. The floor covering, a ribbed linoleum-like material, made it easy to slide heavy cargo in. The author's kids also tended to slide around a lot until he carpeted the floor. With the tailgate up, the cargo floor length was 94.8 inches. The width between wheelhouses was 46.4 inches. The maximum interior height was 32.1 inches.

The 1959 Corvette used these new style slotted wheel covers, which replaced the similar but non-slotted covers of 1958. The two-piece wraparound rear bumpers extended almost as far as the wheel opening.

An assembly line worker is getting a mechanical assist to install the front seat in a 1959 Impala four-door sedan. Note the stacks of floor carpeting in the background. That rear door/quarter panel molding alignment problem will be corrected before the completed car makes it past final inspection.

This is the front compartment of a 1959 Bel Air four-door sedan. The two-tone leather-grain vinyl door trim panel is heavily embossed. The seat fabric is in metallic geometric design pattern cloth. The tunnel area is carpeted and the foot wells are vinyl-coated rubber. That full width instrument panel molding is unique to the Bel Air trim level.

The totally base 1959 Biscayne four-door sedan is not fancy but it's still big. The overall length is 210.9 inches; overall width is 79.9 inches. Assuming this to be a six-cylinder vehicle, the weight is 3,605 pounds. Just two years earlier, the comparable model was 10.9 inches shorter and weighed 364 pounds less.

The third seat of this Kingswood nine-passenger wagon has been folded down for cargo. The second seat remains upright, available for use by passengers. Note the step on the bumper and the courtesy light in the sidewall, both exclusive to the nine-passenger Kingswood, which tipped the scales at a chubby 4,015 pounds. That's a lot of Chevy.

Model 1835, the V-8 Nomad carried the highest advertised price of any 1959 Chevrolet passenger car, $3,009. This one was a 283, which probably had the Powerglide priced at $199.10; power steering $75.35; power brakes, $43.05; deluxe heater, $80.25; Super Turbo-Fire V-8 (four-barrel), $29.10; 8:00 x 14 whitewalls, $35.85; full wheel covers, $24; pushbutton radio with front antenna, $84; and windshield washer, $16.15. The fancy roof mounted luggage carrier was a pricey accessory at $103 and the front bumper grille guard was $31.50. When all these items were totaled, this Nomad had a price tag of $3,730.35. This is probably very close to the way the average Nomad was delivered.

The fuel filler was again relocated in 1959. This time it was behind the hinged license plate holder. The bright bars on the taillight lens tell us we are looking at an Impala. Note that the script to the right of the license plate recess reveals that this car is equipped with Level Air Suspension, a scarce $134.50 option.

The rear-seat passengers in this Impala Sport Coupe had their heads right under that big piece of glass. At 4 p.m. on a hot summer day in Phoenix, that's exactly where you would not want to be. This sport coupe is wearing two-tone paint, wheel covers and whitewalls, all extra cost items.

**'59**

The Biscayne rear passenger compartment was functional but not exactly ostentatious. The seat fabric was spatter pattern cloth. Bolsters were light-tone leather-grain vinyl. The floor covering was a spatter-accented vinyl coated black rubber mat. This interior was available in light and medium gray, light and medium yellow-green and light and medium blue.

An early attempt at the light chassis, big engine muscle car concept resulted in this fast but poorly received 1959 Chevrolet big-block V-8. The engine shown was a 348-cid, 280-hp, Super Turbo-Thrust V-8 featuring three two-barrel carburetors.

Chevrolet's lowest cost station wagon, the two-door, six-passenger Brookwood, is shown here. While the sedans and coupes now employed a fuel filler hidden behind the license plate, the wagons were filled through a door on the left quarter panel.

In December of 1956, this was a proposal for the 1959 Chevrolet. The shape of the windows and contour of the roof suggest that this was based on the 1958 body shell. The side sculpturing and rear bumper have something of a 1959-60 Cadillac look.

This is a good angle from which to view the new 1959 Corvette hood, no longer sporting the rows of simulated louvers, and the now-clean trunk lid. This was a true performance bargain with an advertised price of just $3,875.

The lowest priced six-passenger Chevrolet was this 1959 Biscayne six-cylinder, model 1111. Listing for $2,247, it weighed 3,535 pounds and was 210.9 inches overall. Most of today's drivers would find that a manual steering Biscayne suffers from heavy handling and slow steering.

A 1959 Impala Sport Sedan had a huge trunk. The spare tire stands upright on the right side. The jack can be seen just below the opening. A spatter finish mat was used. While very spacious, the trunk had a very high lift-over. The lack of jacking instructions may indicate that this was a prototype vehicle.

This very artsy advertising shot really shows the Impala-only fender top moldings that flow back from the fender ornaments. Impala decklids also had a molding, which ran the entire length of the center valley. That simulated air exhaust in the roof, while serving no function, is still a nice styling touch.

In this profile view it is apparent why that portion of a vehicle above the belt line is called the "greenhouse." The insurance companies must have been very nervous when they saw the size of the compound-complex windshield they would soon be replacing on the best-selling car in America. The Impala Sport Coupe shown has optional two-tone paint, wheel covers and whitewalls.

This is a model 1635 Parkwood V-8, four-door, six-passenger station wagon. The Parkwood shared Bel Air interior and exterior trim. This 3,970-pound vehicle is shown with optional two-tone paint and whitewalls. Note the interesting non-functional, triangular window between the rear door and the larger quarter glass.

Rear visibility should not have been a problem for the drivers of 1959 El Caminos. The full length Bel Air series body side molding had an ivory stripe. As in the Biscayne series, the fender ornaments were extra-cost options and were not installed on this vehicle. It does have optional whitewalls and a radio.

This 1959 Chevrolet is powered by a 250-hp, 348-cid, Turbo-Thrust V-8 using a four-barrel carburetor. It is also equipped with power steering, power brakes and windshield washer. This shot shows how a wire rod retained the hood blanket.

There is no external identification on the side of this Biscayne four-door sedan to tell us if this is a six-cylinder model 1119 or a V-8 model 1219. Contrary to Chevrolet's practice up to that time, there is no such identifying ornamentation on the rear either. Such identification is found only on the hood. If this is a model 1119, it carried a delivered price of $2,301. No options are shown.

The combination of "Chevrolet" script, V emblem and crossed flags appears on the hood of 348 powered 1959 Chevrolets. When the flags are removed, leaving the V and the "Chevrolet" script, the vehicle has a 283. If just the "Chevrolet" script appears, a 235-cid six-cylinder engine powers the vehicle.

You don't often see the recessed parking/directional lights of a 1959 Corvette in photos as they are tucked way under. This is a fuel-injected vehicle, attested to by the script at the upper rear of the front fender. This Corvette is probably Snowcrest White with an Inca Silver cove area. That two-tone treatment was a bargain at $16.15. The whitewalls were $31.55.

This black Impala Sport Sedan is shown elsewhere in a very trendy shot on a black set. It takes on a somewhat different personality in this outdoor setting at GM Photographic's Royal Oak studio. For some reason, perhaps the lighting, there appears to be a dark center grille bar. That, of course, is not correct.

This solid color Corvette has the removable plastic hardtop. The lack of "Fuel Injection" script on the front fender tells us that this is one of three available 283 carbureted versions. The 2,840-pound Corvette had a 102-inch wheelbase and rode on 6:70 x 15 tires.

This 283 equipped model 1837 Impala Sport Coupe had an advertised price of $2,717. The whitewalls added $31.35; the full wheel covers, $24; two-tone paint, $26.90; for a total of $2,799.25. The average Impala Sport Coupe buyer added a few more unseen items. Powerglide was a $199.10 option. Power steering added $75.35, power brakes, $43.05; deluxe heater, $80.25; and pushbutton radio with front antenna, $84. With a new total of $3,281, the buyer had a well-equipped car by the standards of 1959.

This is a portion of the Chevrolet exhibit at Boston's 1959 Motorama in November 1958. On display at that time were: a Kingswood nine-passenger station wagon, fuel-injected Corvette, Bel Air four-door sedan and Impala Sport Coupe with accessory front bumper grille guard.

This early 1959 Corvette, probably a prototype or pilot-line car, is wearing a 1958 license plate. Corvettes were 72.8 inches wide and stood just 49.2 inches tall with the top down.

The '59 Corvette was essentially a carryover with new wheel covers, restyled upholstery, no trunk irons, and no simulated hood louvers. Production amounted to 9,670.

Unseen in this shot but an important modification was the new rear trailing arms designed to reduce axle tramp on the 2,840 pound 1959 Corvette. The trunk gap is a bit uneven on this vehicle.

**In 1960 this Chevrolet dealer's used car lot featured several 1959 Chevrolet wagons, several 1959 Fords, a 1959 Plymouth wagon, a 1959 Buick and even a 1959 Cadillac.**

1959 Ford Galaxies were almost never seen without whitewalls and wheel covers but this one was purchased to be beat to death at the General Motors Proving Grounds at Milford, Mich., so those frills were omitted.

This is Studebaker's new Lark. It wasn't really an all-new car. In essence, it was a regular size 1958 Studebaker with each end chopped to create a compact car. It was a very successful effort.

This is the standard size Rambler station wagon. This one happens to be a Rebel V-8. Most of these were six-cylinder models. That low rear roof section limited cargo height.

'59

**Plymouth's Belvedere was, in 1959, a mid-level series aimed at the Chevrolet Bel Air. This was the most tasteful model year for Plymouth fins.**

**Ford's Edsel started 1958 as an Oldsmobile competitor but by 1959, this Ranger was priced between the Bel Air and the Impala.**

# 1959 CHEVROLET MODEL CHART

| TYPE | IMPALA | | BEL AIR | | BISCAYNE | | WAGONS | |
|---|---|---|---|---|---|---|---|---|
| | 6 CYL. | 8 CYL. | 6 CYL. | 8 CYL. | 6 CYL. | 8 CYL. | 6 CYL. | 8 CYL. |
| 2-Door Sedan | | | 1511 | 1611 | 1111 | 1211 | | |
| 2-Door Utility Sedan | | | | | 1121 | 1221 | | |
| 4-Door Sedan | 1719 | 1819 | 1519 | 1619 | 1119 | 1219 | | |
| Sport Coupe  (2-dr. hdtp.) | 1737 | 1837 | | | | | | |
| Sport Sedan (4-dr. hdtp.) | 1739 | 1839 | 1539 | 1639 | | | | |
| Convertible | 1767 | 1867 | | | | | | |
| Brookwood 2-Door 6-pass. | | | | | | | 1115 | 1215 |
| Brookwood 4-Door 6-pass. | | | | | | | 1135 | 1235 |
| Parkwood 4-Door 6-pass. | | | | | | | 1535 | 1635 |
| Kingswood 4-Door 9-pass. | | | | | | | 1545 | 1645 |
| Nomad 4-Door 6-pass. | | | | | | | 1735 | 1835 |

# 1959 EXTERIOR SPECIFICATION COMPARISONS OF FOUR-DOOR SEDANS

| | CHEVROLET BISCAYNE | FORD CUSTOM 300 | PLYMOUTH SAVOY | RAMBLER 6 DELUXE | STUDEBAKER LARK |
|---|---|---|---|---|---|
| Wheelbase | 119.0" | 118.0" | 118.0" | 108.0" | 108.5" |
| Overall Length | 210.9" | 208.0" | 210.0" | 191.0" | 175.0" |
| Front Overhang | 32.6" | 34.2" | 34.3" | 32.0" | 26.4" |
| Rear Overhang | 59.3" | 55.8" | 57.7" | 51.2" | 40.06" |
| Height (design load) | 56.0" | 56.0" | 56.6" | 58.0" | 57.5" |
| Width | 79.9" | 76.8" | 78.0" | 72.2" | 71.3" |
| Tread-front | 60.3" | 59.0" | 60.9" | 57.75" | 57.4" |
| Tread-rear | 59.3" | 56.4" | 59.6" | 58.0" | 56.6" |
| Weight (curb) | 3,605 lbs. | 3,227 lbs. | 3,275 lbs. | 2,934 lbs. | 2,605 lbs. |
| Turning Diameter (wall to wall – max.) | 43.6 ft. | 43.53 ft. | 45.1 ft. | 39.3 ft. | 40.0 ft. |

# 1959 INTERIOR ROOM COMPARISONS OF FOUR-DOOR SEDANS

| | CHEVROLET BISCAYNE | FORD CUSTOM 300 | PLYMOUTH SAVOY | RAMBLER 6 DELUXE | STUDEBAKER LARK |
|---|---|---|---|---|---|
| Front Headroom | 36.1" | 33.8" | 35.7" | 36.0" | 36.0" |
| Rear Headroom | 34.3" | 33.5" | 34.2" | 35.0" | 35.0" |
| Front Legroom | 45.0" | 42.8" | 45.5" | 43.0" | 44.0" |
| Rear Legroom | 42.8" | 40.4" | 41.5" | 40.0" | 41.0" |
| Front Shoulder Room | 60.5" | 56.7" | 60.5" | 57.7" | 55.5" |
| Rear Shoulder Room | 59.7" | 57.0" | 60.4" | 57.6" | 54.5" |
| Front Hip Room | 66.1" | 60.4" | 63.0" | 59.8" | 59.5" |
| Rear Hip Room | 65.5" | 60.8" | 62.7" | 60.1" | 59.0" |

# 1959 CHEVROLET ENGINE CHART

| ENGINE | HP @ RPM | TORQUE @ RPM |
|---|---|---|
| 235.5 c.i.d. Base 6 | 135 @ 4000 | 217 @ 2000-2400 |
| 283 c.i.d. 2-bbl. V-8 | 185 @ 4600 | 275 @ 2400 |
| 348 c.i.d. V-8 | 250 @ 4400 | 355 @ 2800 |
| 283 c.i.d. 4-bbl. V-8 | 230 @ 4800 | 300 @ 3000 |
| 283 c.i.d. Fuel Injection V-8 | 250 @ 5000 | 305 @ 3800 |
| 283 c.i.d. Fuel Injection V-8* | 290 @ 6200 | 290 @ 4500 |
| 348 c.i.d. 4-bbl. V-8* | 305 @ 5600 | 350 @ 3600 |
| 348 c.i.d. 3x2-bbl. V-8 | 280 @ 4800 | 355 @ 3200 |
| 348 c.i.d. 3x2-bbl. V-8* | 335 @ 5800 | 362 @ 3600 |
| 348 c.i.d. 4-bbl. V-8* | 320 @ 5600 | 358 @ 3600 |

* Special Camshaft

# 1959 FORD ENGINE CHART

| ENGINE | HP @ RPM | TORQUE @ RPM |
|---|---|---|
| 223 c.i.d. Base 6 | 145 @ 4000 | 206 @ 2200 |
| 292 c.i.d. 2-bbl. V-8 | 200 @ 4400 | 285 @ 2200 |
| 332 c.i.d. 2-bbl. V-8 | 225 @ 4400 | 325 @ 2200 |
| 352 c.i.d. 4-bbl. V-8 | 300 @ 4600 | 380 @ 2800 |

# 1959 PLYMOUTH ENGINE CHART

| ENGINE | HP @ RPM | TORQUE @ RPM |
|---|---|---|
| 230 c.i.d. Base 6 | 132 @ 3600 | 205 @ 1200 |
| 318 c.i.d. 2-bbl. V-8 | 230 @ 4400 | 340 @ 2400 |
| 318 c.i.d. 4-bbl. V-8 | 260 @ 4400 | 345 @ 2800 |
| 361 c.i.d. 4-bbl. V-8 | 305 @ 4600 | 395 @ 3000 |

# 1959 CHEVROLET CORVETTE ENGINE CHART

| ENGINE | HP @ RPM | TORQUE @ RPM |
|---|---|---|
| 283 c.i.d. 4-bbl. V-8 | 230 @ 4800 | 300 @ 3000 |
| 283 c.i.d. 2x4-bbl. V-8 | 245 @ 5000 | 300 @ 3800 |
| 283 c.i.d. 2x4-bbl. V-8* | 270 @ 6000 | 285 @ 4200 |
| 283 c.i.d. Fuel Injection V-8 | 250 @ 5000 | 305 @ 3800 |
| 283 c.i.d. Fuel Injection V-8* | 290 @ 6200 | 290 @ 4400 |

* Special Camshaft

# 1959 RAMBLER ENGINE CHART

| ENGINE | HP @ RPM | TORQUE @ RPM |
|--------|----------|--------------|
| 195.6 c.i.d. Base 6 | 127 @ 4200 | 180 @ 1600 |
| 195.6 c.i.d. 2-bbl. 6 | 138 @ 4500 | 185 @ 1800 |
| 250 c.i.d. 4-bbl. V-8 | 215 @ 4900 | 260 @ 2500 |

# 1959 STUDEBAKER LARK ENGINE CHART

| ENGINE | HP @ RPM | TORQUE @ RPM |
|--------|----------|--------------|
| 169.6 c.i.d. Base 6 | 90 @ 4000 | 145 @ 2000 |
| 259.2 c.i.d. 2-bbl. V-8 | 180 @ 4500 | 260 @ 2800 |
| 259.2 c.i.d. 4-bbl. V-8 | 195 @ 4500 | 265 @ 3000 |

# 1959 CHEVROLET COLOR CHART

- Grecian Gray
- Satin Beige
- Crown Sapphire
- Tuxedo Black
- Snowcrest White
- Harbor Blue
- Cameo Coral
- Gothic Gold
- Classic Cream
- Aspen Green
- Highland Green
- Frost Blue
- Roman Red

- Tuxedo Black/Snowcrest White
- Frost Blue/Harbor Blue
- Highland Green/Snowcrest White
- Cameo Coral/Satin Beige
- Classic Cream/Aspen Green
- Harbor Blue/Frost Blue
- Crown Sapphire/Snowcrest White
- Roman Red/Snowcrest White
- Grecian Gray/Snowcrest White
- Gothic Gold/Satin Beige

# 1959 CHEVROLET CORVETTE COLOR CHART

SOLID COLORS

- Tuxedo Black
- Crown Sapphire
- Inca Silver
- Classic Cream
- Roman Red
- Frost Blue
- Snowcrest White

TWO-TONE COLORS

- Tuxedo Black/Inca Silver
- Classic Cream/Snowcrest White
- Frost Blue/Snowcrest White
- Crown Sapphire/Snowcrest White
- Roman Red/Snowcrest White
- Snowcrest White/Inca Silver
- Inca Silver/Snowcrest White

## 60

Alex Nicholas (glasses and tie) was the first Chevrolet representative I met when I joined Jam
Handy in 1969. He was representing Chevrolet Engineering Product Information on the location
shoot, in Albuquerque, New Mexico, of the 1970 Chevrolet announcement film. Alex was the
engineer who managed the build of the early photographic vehicles and dealt them out to agency
guys like myself. Alex became a friend and was totally professional as I dealt with him while
working with Chevrolet at three different agencies. Here, he is directing the prepping of a 1960
Impala, possibly at the dealer announcement show.

# 1960: Innovative Corvair debuts, Chevy #1

T he auto industry had seen some unusual things happen in the last few years of the 1950s. The evolution of domestic cars in 1953 through 1956 was predictable. There were economic spurts and retrenchments but, in general, the American public was basking in a cheerful euphoria under the benevolent and fatherly leadership of Ike. The president was busy addressing plans for an interstate highway system that would carry the public rapidly over smooth and well-engineered ribbons of concrete. The public liked the idea and demanded more powerful automobiles that would be able to travel great distances at high speeds, hour after hour, without mechanical meltdown. Modern overhead valve V-8 engines were popping up everywhere. Suspension and steering systems were being updated to provide safe, stable handling to help insure that these more powerful

vehicles wouldn't go flying off those fast new roads.

The '50s was a time of unrestrained color applications with tri-tones popping up and otherwise manly men buying cars in shades of pink, turquoise, purple and even lavender. Longer, lower and wider were words used to describe the most purchased or most admired vehicles of the day. Interiors were becoming totally color coordinated and the new fabrics were quite fanciful. Planned obsolescence was never more in synch with the mood of the public. By 1955, for example, a 1952 Chevrolet or 1952 Dodge looked pretty dreary in comparison to a new model of the same make.

As the American industry rode a heady wave of public approval, there was a quiet but growing wave of public revolt developing on a parallel road. It was a small rebellion at first and those weird little European imports were thought to be doing no more than catching crumbs falling off the table. The public, it seemed, was encouraging the industry to build lower, longer, wider, heavier, and more radically styled cars. When Chevrolet got a little more conservative, failed to get longer, lower, wider like Ford and Plymouth in 1957, the public elevated Ford to first place in sales.

Concurrently, splinters from that same public body were ignoring Chevrolets, available for immediate delivery, to place orders for scarce VWs. There was a big new Chevy and styling blunders at Ford in 1958. Chevy did a little victory dance over Ford and everybody now knew somebody who had a VW – and loved it. Most of those VW owners became rabid fans, "unpaid salesmen" is not an unreasonable description. Even normal people

The lowest-priced regular-size Chevrolet was this Biscayne Utility two-door sedan six-cylinder model 1121. The Utility Sedan had a level platform covering the rear floor and seat area to provide an inside storage area. The advertised price of the Utility two-door sedan was $2,175.

were starting to buy those silly little cars. This was getting really strange. The public snubbed big domestic models that didn't look big enough. At the same time an ever increasing body of car buyers was electing much smaller, much less powerful, odd looking, rather pricey European cars or George Romney's sensible Ramblers. Many of these buyers wouldn't test drive a Ford or Chevy. The industry tried to respond with some of its own captive imports but that wasn't the answer. It appeared that the industry was going to need to provide a domestic product to satisfy the desires of the traditional buyer and yet another to intercept those buyers who were splintering off to buy small cars. 1960 was the year those new compact cars would arrive in Chevrolet, Ford, Plymouth and Mercury dealerships.

Chevrolet's controversial all-new styling had helped outsell Ford in 1959, but not by much. This year, 1960, that body was facelifted and simplified to result in a less radical design. Viewed from the front, the new 1960 Chevrolet featured a new oval grille incorporating a series of fine horizontal bars bisected by a single wide bar incorporating an oval surrounding a central emblem that told the knowledgeable which engine was hidden within. A stand-alone Chevrolet crest signified a six-cylinder. A silver V was added to the crest on 283 models. If the V was gold you were looking at a 348. Gone were the long, screened openings in the hood which critics had called "nostrils." The low, flat hood now flowed to the grille's upper edge and incorporated a pair of windsplits, which probably served to reduce flexing in that huge panel. At the hood's leading edge, individual chrome block letters spelled out

"CHEVROLET." The slim bumper was carried high with large wraparound wing tips. The crowned central section formed integral guards at each end of a ribbed and recessed argent finished license panel. Body color valance panels located beneath the bumper now carried the parking/turn signal lamps. A slender, canted character line rose from the leading edge of the front fender, flowing through the doors to form the outer edge of the now-squared-off horizontal fin. Side sculpturing on the quarter panel and rear door was given more definition with a pair of crisp horizontal lines. At the rear there was no trace of the cat's-eyes taillights. Above the bumper a full-width horizontal panel housed round taillights and, on the Impala, back-up lights flanked the recessed license pocket. The license plate pulled down to reveal the centered fuel filler. There had been complaints about the high lift-over of the 1959 Chevrolet trunk. The new rear styling with a lower luggage compartment sill featured a wider, lower center section for easier loading and unloading of luggage and cargo.

The 1960 Chevrolet was, for the most part, a refinement of the 1959 model. The 1959 was an all-new body on a slightly modified chassis which had been all new in 1958. Additional chassis modifications were performed for 1960. These were of the magnitude of larger front brake cylinders that increased the front wheels' share of braking effort, reducing the possibility of rear wheel skidding for safer straight-line stops. In keeping with Chevrolet's desire to add appeal to the buyer of more expensive brands, cruise control was added to the option list with a price tag of $93.50. Autronic Eye was replaced by a new, functionally

'60

The 1960 Impala Sport Coupe was "toned-down" to satisfy the critics who felt the 1959 version was too gimmicky. The smooth flowing fins were squared off, side trim was simplified and taillights became less prominent.

improved, headlamp beam control known as Guide Matic. The parking brake mechanism was re-designed to eliminate pedal-kickback. The power steering pump was separated from the generator and was now independently mounted. Frame modifications included a new cross member, which improved rear suspension durability while increasing frame rigidity. The rubber body mounts were also modified to improve the isolation of body from frame. Frame modifications also made it possible to lower and narrow the front floor tunnel (transmission hump) for improved front passenger foot room.

For the first time since 1957, no fuel-injected engines appeared in the passenger car engine chart although fuel injection was still an attraction for Corvette buyers. The entry-level engine continued to be the 234 cid Hi Thrift 6, still rated at 135 horsepower at 4,000 rpm.

In a move designed to appeal to the economy minded buyer who wanted the flexibility and smooth response of a V-8, Chevrolet introduced the Economy Turbo Fire V-8. The Economy Turbo Fire was a mild cam version of the 283 two-barrel V-8 with an 8.5:1 compression ratio. In that this was the base V-8 and the only two-barrel V-8 in the line, this was a very popular powerplant in spite of a relatively low horsepower of 170 at 4,200 rpm (torque: 275 lbs.-ft. at 2,200).

The 283 cid four-barrel Super Turbo Fire V-8 with 9.5:1 compression ratio made 230 horses at 4,800 rpm (torque: 300 lbs.-ft. at 3,000 rpm).

Now in its third year, and with the fuel-injection engines out of the mix, the 348 cid big block Turbo Thrust family of engines became the obvious choice of the performance minded. The four-barrel Turbo Thrust turned out 250 horses at 4,400 rpm (torque: 355 lbs.-ft. at 2,800 rpm).

The Super Turbo Thrust V-8 used three two-barrel carburetors to produce 280 horses at 4,800 rpm. These engines featured a 9.5:1 compression ratio. With the addition of a special camshaft, high-speed valve train with mechanical lifters, an 11.25:1 compression ratio and extra-heavy-duty components, these 348s packed some serious power. The four-barrel Turbo Thrust Special kicked out 305 horses at 5,200 rpm and was used in combination with a heavy-duty Powerglide.

When combined with three-speed or four-speed synchromesh transmissions, the four-barrel Turbo Thrust Special made 320 horses at 5,600 rpm. The Super Turbo Thrust Special, featuring three two-barrel carburetors, developed 335 horses at 5,800 rpm with three-speed or four-speed synchromesh transmissions.

The regular Chevrolet was available in four series; Impala, Bel Air and Biscayne with a line of wagons in corresponding trim levels. As in 1959, the Impala was the top-of-the-line series. For 1960 Impalas were offered in four body styles; four-door sedan, Sport Sedan (four-door hardtop), Sport Coupe (two-door hardtop), and Convertible. Impala interiors were a mix of carryover and new features. The Corvette-inspired instrument panel and sports-type steering wheel were carried over for 1960 with the Impala trim level again

This talented lady is standing on a 1960 Bel Air Sport Coupe (a new model this year) and a 1960 Corvair 700 four-door sedan while effortlessly supporting a 1960 Impala Sport Sedan and a 1960 Corvair 500 four-door sedan. The Corvair exterior trim level differences can be seen.

featuring a bright embossed facing over the entire lower half of the panel. Electric clock, cigarette lighter, chrome-capped control knobs and parking brake alarm were among the quality features. While utilizing the same basic seats, the seat sew pattern and fabrics were totally new. Seat inserts now featured a two-tone pattern nylon-faced cloth in a houndstooth check pattern. This pattern, printed on vinyl, was used on convertible seats and as an accent on all Impala door panels, which were also restyled to compliment the new seat design. The large, bright aluminum front seat end panels were carried over from 1959. The rear seat backrest of two-door models still featured the recessed speaker grille that became an Impala trademark in 1958. The long armrests, used on all doors, were also continued from 1959, still incorporating the paddle-type door handle and safety reflectors and, in the rear, individual ashtrays. Wall-to-wall carpet was standard with all closed Impalas. Carpet was mixed with colored vinyl-coated rubber in convertibles. Six interior trim colors were available for every Impala model; white and black, light and medium green, light and medium blue, light and medium copper, light and medium copper, light and medium turquoise, and white and red. If Chevrolet couldn't supply a 1960 Impala with your favorite interior color, it wasn't because it didn't try.

Following the lead of Impala, the Bel Air interiors were essentially those of 1959 with new fabrics and sew patterns. The instrument panel's full width bright molding was carried over from 1959 Bel Airs. The two spoke steering wheel and horn ring were also carryover items. The new seating surfaces were trimmed in a tri-tone nylon stripe cloth. Seat bolsters were of leather-grain vinyl. Armrests were supplied front and rear (integral in design of Sport Coupe rear sidewall) with the rear incorporating ashtrays. Door panel and sidewall trim were in two-tone vinyl with a single bright molding and stamped embossments. The floor carpet was again a carryover combination of carpet and vinyl-coated rubber. Five interior trim color combinations were offered for all Bel Air models; light and dark gray, light and medium green, light and medium blue, light and medium copper, and light and medium turquoise.

Biscayne interiors were the least changed for 1960. The twin-cove instrument panel and two-spoke steering wheel were identical to those of 1959 except that the slender oval ornament in the passenger side cove was deleted for 1960. The door trim panels and sidewalls received a higher color break and modified embossed character lines. Colored vinyl coated rubber mats covered front and rear floors. Standard equipment now included armrests (on front doors only) and two sun visors. The seating surfaces were upholstered in an attractive nylon-faced pattern cloth with bolsters done in light-tone leather-grain vinyl. Biscayne two-door and four-door sedans were offered in three trim color combinations: silver and gray, light and medium green, and light and medium blue. Silver and gray was the sole trim offered for the utility sedan.

For 1960, Chevrolet exterior trim was extensively modified for all series. Impala models featured almost all-new trim. Front fender trim was simplified. A slender bright molding at mid-headlight level flowed from the

The Biscayne four-door sedan was Chevrolet's lowest priced regular size four-door. This is a model 1119 six-cylinder version. The crest in the decklid identifies a six-cylinder. If the crest is nested in a V, you are looking at a V-8. The advertised price of this vehicle was $2,316. While it has a radio, there are no exterior options or accessories.

grille opening to the wheel opening. Four slim diecast bar ornaments with a black paint fill were stacked near, two over and two under, the larger front fender molding. Midway on the front door character line, a concave area housed the bright molding, which tapered to the rear to outline the fin area terminating on the decklid. The most distinguishing Impala trim was the contrasting color insert, which ran the full length of the quarter panel and part of the rear door on four-door models. This insert covered about 7/8 of two-door quarter panels. Narrow moldings ran over and under the contrasting color band, flowing back from a large ornament described by Chevrolet as "missile styled." An "Impala" script and emblem were housed in this area. Bright moldings edged the roof and belt on closed models. The high mounted simulated exhaust vent of the 1959 models was replaced by a simulated vent incorporated in the reveal molding beneath the rear window. At the rear the full-width taillight panel was outlined and faced in bright aluminum with new triple rear light units, including circular dual taillights plus back-up lights. Stop and directional signal functions were served by the outer units.

The Bel Air line consisted of four models: two-door sedan, four-door sedan, Sport Sedan (four-door hardtop), and Sport Coupe (two-door hardtop). Chevrolet had been rather undecided about the issue of mid-level hardtops with the Bel Air Sport Sedan being the only such vehicle in 1959. For 1960, the Sport Coupe was added to the Bel Air line. Bel Airs, of course, wore somewhat less jewelry than Impalas. For the first time in

Bel Air history, there were no side moldings gracing the front fenders. There was only a "Bel Air" script and crest on the front fender. The bright character line fill of the Impala trim level carried over to Bel Air. The quarter panel's contrasting color insert and dual side moldings were replaced by a single slim molding, which flowed back from the "missile" side ornament. The Sport Coupe and conventional sedans featured a bright drip rail molding. Belt moldings were not employed. The dual circular taillights were placed in the recessed cove, which was outlined by a bright aluminum molding. Back-up lights were extra cost and carried outside the cove under the rear bumper. The cove was finished in roof color. The Impala's simulated exhaust vents were not included on Bel Airs.

The three model Biscayne series again held down the entry-level position among regular Chevrolets. In addition to the four-door sedan and two-door sedan, the Biscayne line also included the Utility Sedan. Like the Utility Sedan of 1959, this vehicle featured a flat platform where one would generally find the rear seat. The Bel Air didn't offer a lot of trim to delete when building the Biscayne. The Bel Air front fender script and crest were replaced by a "Biscayne" script, no crest. The bright character line fill, which originated on the front door of the Impala and Bel Air, was continued by Biscayne but was thinner. It was described in the Chevrolet dealer album thusly: "Slim-styled rear deck tailplane outline moldings." The "missile-wing" quarter panel ornament was a modified version of that used on the Bel Air and was not accompanied by the slim

A new model for 1960, this Bel Air sport Coupe is a 283 V-8 as attested to by the decklid V accompanied by a crest. Bel Air level trim included the molding surrounding the rear cove area, the single quarter panel molding, and simplified front fender trim.

quarter panel molding that distinguished the Bel Air. Missing also was the bright molding, which outlined the taillight panel. On the plus side, the Biscayne did retain the bright windshield and rear window moldings, ventipane frames and posts and taillight frames.

Station wagons continued to be in high demand among America's families. Following the precedent of previous years, Chevrolet wagons were treated as a separate series with trim levels corresponding to Impala, Bel Air and Biscayne. Once again, the top-of-the-line Nomad, corresponding to the Impala, was available only as a six-passenger vehicle. Two models, the nine-passenger Kingswood and the six-passenger Parkwood, wore Bel Air trim. At the entry level, trimmed like the Biscayne, was a pair of six-passenger Brookwood wagons. One of those Brookwoods was Chevrolet's only two-door station wagon. In this carryover year, there wasn't anything new in terms of station wagon technology but last year's Chevrolet wagons had some advanced features that kept the 1960 models current. Wagons were intended to carry stuff. "Stuff" could be cargo or it could be people, and the measure of a good wagon was how well it handled "stuff." The beautiful Nomads of 1955, '56 and '57 had not been very good at dealing with a lot of cargo and, because of that, and the high price, wagon buyers went with more practical models. The 1960 Chevrolet wagons were very practical wagons with squared-off rear ends, which allowed longer loads at belt level and at roof level, not just at the floor. The roll-down rear window increased versatility and eliminated the restrictive upper tailgate. Second

seats folded flat with one easy operation and passengers in the rear-facing third seat sat on real cushions, not removable mats that were intended to be rolled up and stowed someplace when not in use. And yet, Chevrolet wagons managed to look stylish and contemporary. Neat trick. Nice wagons.

*Road & Track* magazine stirred up Corvette fans in 1959 with predictions of big changes for 1960. Identified as the Q-model, this lighter, smaller sports car would feature a transaxle and dramatic new styling. As it turned out, the 1960 Corvette was visually unchanged from the 1959 update of the 1958 model. Under the sporty fiberglass skin, the Corvette continued to improve, mostly in ways that were too sophisticated for the average driver to notice. In an ongoing program to improve handling through better weight distribution, the use of aluminum was increased in power train components such as the clutch housing for synchromesh transmissions. An aluminum radiator was included with the two top engine options. Cylinder heads on fuel-injected engines were also aluminum. Brake system changes boosted front wheel braking for improved straight-line stops.

As in previous years, all 1960 Corvette engines were 283 V-8s. There were five engines available: the entry level, lowest power unit was the four-barrel which made 230 horses at 4,800 rpm (torque: 300 lbs.-ft at 3,000 rpm).

The 283 V-8 with two four-barrels developed 245 horses at 5,000 rpm (torque: 300 lbs.-ft. at 3,800 rpm).

The Chevrolet's lowest price wagon for 1960 was this model 1115 (six-cylinder) or 1215 (V-8) two-door, six-passenger station wagon. In the side view, trim was limited to the quarter panel "missile" and a thin molding in the recessed upper character line. In six-cylinder form, the model 1115 had an advertised price of $2,586.

The 283 V-8 with two four-barrels when equipped with special cam, mechanical lifters and special valves was good for 270 horses at 6,000 rpm (torque: 285 lbs.-ft. at 4,200 rpm).

The 283 V-8 Fuel Injected engine with hydraulic lifters made 250 horses at 5,200 rpm (torque: 305 lbs.-ft. at 4,400 rpm).

The 283 V-8 Fuel Injected engine with special cam, special valves and mechanical lifters turned out 290 horses at 6,200 rpm (torque: 295 lbs.-ft. at 4,700-5,100 rpm).

The two-speed Powerglide was available with the 230 horsepower and 245 horsepower engines only. All engines could be had with three-speed close-ratio synchromesh or four-speed close ratio synchromesh transmission.

Not all Corvettes were sold to people who cared about such things as weight distribution and mechanical lifters. A growing number of Corvette buyers were more concerned about looking good. And Chevrolet took care of them too. 1960 Corvettes were offered in eight solid colors. The cove area could be painted either white or silver to create the eight available two-tone combinations. Medium-tone leather grain vinyl interiors were available in four colors and convertible tops could be specified in any of three colors.

The biggest excitement in the automotive world of 1960 was generated by the long-awaited compact cars from America's Big Three, General Motors, Ford and Chrysler. Each had carefully studied the American public's new small car buying habits. Starting with a fresh sheet of paper, they began to develop small cars for American-size people to drive in American cities and on the new American interstate highways. The goal was to offer the most desirable attributes of the popular imports, including fuel economy, ease of handling, simplicity of design and low initial cost. These attributes were to be compromised as little as possible while providing room for an American family of six. The acceleration was to be sprightly enough, and the cruising speed high enough, to be compatible with American driving habits while offering attractive fuel economy. The styling was to be fresh but not radical. The domestic manufacturers had pretty much driven public tastes for decades and each knew exactly what the public needed. Of the three new vehicles, the Chevrolet Corvair was by far the most innovative.

The American public was, by now, very familiar with the 1930s looking VW. Most knew that the engine was in the rear and quite a few knew that they were air-cooled. The advertising had stressed the remarkable things a VW would do in snow and sand. Word of mouth had it that these things were even more dependable than they were economical. Chevrolet and GM executives were convinced that it made good sense to capitalize on VW's pioneering efforts. The public, they reasoned was familiar with the concepts of rear engines and air-cooling. They also reasoned that, given a choice, that same public would like a car that would carry six persons in comfort. They also knew that the public would really go wild if the car were actually styled. So it

This 1960 Impala Sport Sedan is powered by a 348 V-8. When a crossed flags emblem is used with the decklid V, the vehicle is powered by a 348. The Impala exterior trim includes a bright and black vertically embossed taillight cove applique and triple taillight units. Twin moldings flow back from the large, door mounted "missile" style ornament. An Impala script and crossed flags are located between the moldings.

came to pass that the Chevrolet economy car would be an air-cooled rear-engine design, new from the ground-up with a capacity for six passengers and some luggage. The car was to be styled in the best of GM tradition.

At announcement time the Corvair was available as only a four-door sedan in base 500 series or up-level 700 series. At 108 inches the Corvair's wheelbase placed it in the ranks of the larger of small cars. In comparison, the VW's wheelbase was 94.5 inches and the Rambler American's was 100 inches. The Chevrolet dealer album for 1960 gave an insight into Chevrolet's view of the market and its new car: "Nine years in development, the completely new Chevrolet Corvair is specifically engineered to be everything a compact car should be with no compromising use of existing designs and components.

The Corvair embodies important advances in every major phase of automotive design, economy, ride roominess, handling ease, and overall roadability. A revolutionary new power unit is located at the rear away from the passenger compartment. The floor is virtually flat, with ample foot room for all passengers. Engineered weight distribution gives this new compact car exceptional traction, easier steering, surer stopping, and a wonderfully smooth constant ride."

"From the very outset, the Corvair was designed specifically to American standards of six-passenger comfort, performance and safety. Exhaustive tests and development procedures have proved every principle and detail – Corvair is America's most completely tested new car. Only Chevrolet could bring together the

resources, creative engineering and technical skills to produce such a car – it's Chevrolet's proud pioneer in the newest American Automotive tradition." Wow! After 40 years it still sounds exciting. And of course, it was truly exciting at the time.

The heart of this new design was the "Unipack Power Team." Unipack, according to Chevrolet, referred to the packaging of major components in an "integrated unit of engine, transmission, and final drive, combining economy, compactness, and spirited performance to a degree never before possible." The horizontally opposed "Turbo-Air" six-cylinder was light in weight – about half that of a conventional six-cylinder engine, and very compact. The crankcase and cylinder heads were cast of aluminum alloy. Individually cast ferrous alloy cylinders were deeply finned for effective cooling. Hydraulic valve lifters were employed. Twin one-barrel carburetors delivered fuel to each bank of cylinders, sharing a single, central air cleaner. The automatic choke was located at the air cleaner inlet kept fuel-air mixture balanced.

Cooling was provided by a blower centered above the engine crankcase to draw cooling air into the engine compartment through louvers in the lid and force it downward through the engine to exit through the exhaust grille beneath the rear bumper. The 140-cid Turbo-Air made 80 horsepower at 4,400 rpm (torque: 125 lbs.-ft. at 2,400 rpm).

The transaxle combined all transmission and rear axle gearing. With the conventional rear axle eliminated, the final drive gearing-ring gear, pinion, and differential – was located between the clutch (with manual

General Motors Photographic created an indoor set at its Royal Oak studio representing the gates of the famed Greenbriar. This 1960 Nomad was shot on that set. The Nomad shared the Impala trim level. This trim level included special moldings between the grille and front wheel openings and a pair of bar ornaments over, and another pair under, the molding. Bright moldings edged the roof, beltline and quarter windows.

transmission) or torque converter (Powerglide) and transmission gearbox.

Like the VW and, in fact, most of the world's small cars, the Corvair featured unitized construction. In this type of construction, the body was designed in such a way that it was possible to eliminate the traditional frame. It made sense, especially in a small car where the benefits of lightweight and inherent strength were most appreciated. The Corvair's independent front and rear suspensions were unit-assembled on strong crossmembers that were then bolted to the unitized body structure. Each corner was supported by a coil spring.

At announcement time, the interior of even the top-of-the-line Corvair 700 was too spartan for the taste of the target market. The 500 trim level had the cheapest looking interior since the Henry J. Somehow Chevrolet's product people got the idea that the public expected "compact" to be the equivalent of "cheap." The door trim was similar to that used in pickup trucks where a panel was inserted in the body-color door inner structure. The instrument panel was designed and assembled in such a way that the instrument cluster, radio and glove box had a hang-on look. Even the 700 model lacked a horn ring and floor covering in both series was rubber mat-black on 500, colored on 700. For those buyers of 500 or 700 models who wanted front armrests, right sunvisor or a cigarette lighter, the Deluxe Body equipment group was offered. The author, with the skill of your average Monday morning quarterback, believes that the 700 should have been the base trim level and the up level should have been trimmed like a

contemporary Bel Air. The extra cost would have been negligible. Remember that Chevrolet's success was built on the Sloan principle of charging a little more money for a noticeably nicer car. It's a shame that the first Corvair that millions of Americans saw was not as desirable as it would eventually be when the 900 series Monza arrived in mid-1960.

Corvair exteriors were clean and simple. The lines were so pure that the almost trim-free 500 looked pretty good. The 700 added a thin bright molding, which completely encircled the car just below the belt line. The windshield and back glass each received a bright reveal molding and a rain rail molding capped off the bright work package.

When the Corvair arrived in October 1959, the sole body style was the four-door sedan. The Club Coupe was added to both series in January. The coupe was a sporty little car with a long rear deck and full rear wheel openings. In May, the 900 series Monza Club Coupe was released. The Monza's well-trimmed interior featured vinyl bucket seats with bright accents. The exterior trim changes included the deletion of the belt molding and the addition of rocker moldings and other exterior bright touches. It was the Monza that began to define the sporty image that would eventually characterize the Corvair. The Monza example is typical of Chevrolet's ability to identify a product problem early and apply an appropriate fix on a timely basis.

While the Corvair was conceived to combat the influx of European imports, the reality is that the real competition always had been, and still was, Ford. Ford's

The Impala Convertible displayed its squared-off "tail planes" and deep side sculpturing. The deck-lid mounted crossed flags tell us that this vehicle had a 348 V-8. Looking like a big car, this Impala was 210.8 inches overall and weighed 3,635 pounds.

approach to the compact car was more conventional. A water-cooled, front-engine vehicle on a 109.5-inch wheelbase. Overall length was 109.5 inches, 1.5 inches longer than Corvair. The unitized body Falcon was basically a scaled-down version of a big American car. While the Corvair was aimed at the segment that was impressed by innovative engineering, the Falcon addressed the growing number of Americans who felt that cars had become unnecessarily large. The folks that were not willing to buy a car that was clumsy to drive and park and cost too much to operate. This was, of course, the audience to which George Romney of American Motors had been preaching. The 1960 Falcon catalog preached verse and scripture to these automotive Pilgrims; "You can forget about power brakes and power steering. You simply don't need them in this new-size Ford."

The Falcon was powered by an all-new 90 hp, 144.5-cid in-line six-cylinder OHV engine which could be teamed with a three-speed manual transmission or two-speed automatic. Ford claimed up to 30 mpg on regular gas. This claim may have been possible but that was much better than the average driver got out of the average Falcon. The front suspension employed coil springs while leaf springs were used in the rear. The Falcon design was simple and clean with plenty of glass to give a light, airy look. It also looked rather tall and narrow. It would come as no surprise to learn that the Falcon was taller than the Corvair by 3.2 inches. It is, however, very surprising to learn that the Falcon was actually 3.4 inches wider than the Corvair. Falcons had

6.00 x 13 tires, smaller than the 6.50 x 13 tires standard on Corvair and that, plus the Falcon's unusually high ride height, contributed to a "spindly" look.

The Falcon was offered in just one basic series but it was possible to create a higher level model by ordering the deluxe trim package. The base interior in light and dark gray was roughly the visual equivalent of the Corvair 700. The Deluxe package included pleated tweed nylon seat inserts and door panel trim in three colors. This package also added a deluxe white steering wheel with horn ring, rear armrests, ashtrays and more. Also included were bright upper doorframe moldings and taillight rings. Other dress-up accessories were available to elevate the Falcon to a level that early Corvairs couldn't touch.

Conceptually the Corvair and Falcon were very different but in size they were quite similar. The Falcon's wheelbase and overall length exceeded those of the Corvair by 1.2 inches and 1.5 inches respectively. The Falcon was about 50 pounds heavier. Front and rear headroom and front legroom numbers were close. The Falcon had big advantages in rear legroom and rear shoulder room. The Corvair had the edge in front hip room.

At mid-year, the Falcon launched a pair of station wagons, a two-door and a four-door. Bigger and heavier than the sedans, but sharing the same engines and transmissions, the new wagons looked better than they performed.

Chrysler's entry into the compact car field was the

The front sheet metal (front clip) is being lowered onto the frame of a 1960 Chevrolet Parkwood. Four men are carefully guiding the unit to avoid paint damage. A fifth worker in the pit prepares to install the lower bolts and tighten them with an air wrench.

Valiant. Later officially known as the Plymouth Valiant, at introduction it was not a Plymouth. While the Corvair was a radical exercise in engineering and the Falcon was a very conservative approach to downsizing the conventional car, the Valiant was a conventional car that bristled with innovative engineering and styling concepts. Right out of the box, the Valiant was a very hated or very adored car. The press described the styling as European. It was certainly different from its trapezoidal grille to its simulated spare tire cover on the semi-fastback decklid. Full wheel cutouts, deep body sculpturing and canted taillights; Virgil Exner's stylists had had a field day. The engineers had some fun too. Valiant had Chrysler's first OHV six-cylinder engine – and it was almost lying on its side. To be exact, the engine tilted 30 degrees to the right for adequate clearance under a low hood. The slant 6, as it was called, was fairly large at 170 cid. The slant 6 made 101 horses at 4,400 rpm (torque: 155 lbs.-ft. at 2,400 rpm). The standard transmission was a three-speed manual. The available automatic was a three-speed Torqueflite. The combination of larger engine and three-speed automatic made for a more spirited little car. Another innovation was Valiant's use of the alternator, replacing the conventional generator.

Like the Corvair and Falcon, the Valiant featured unitized construction. Unlike the others, the Valiant adopted torsion bar front suspension. Valiants were rather heavy at 2,725 pounds, 300 pounds heavier than Falcon. Perhaps it was because of the added weight or maybe just a difference in marketing philosophy,

whatever, Chrysler elected to offer optional power steering and power brakes for the Valiant. Valiants looked big but the wheelbase was actually 1.5 inches shorter than the Corvair's, although overall length was 3.7 inches greater. The Valiant was also offered as a four-door station wagon in two and three-seat versions. If the Valiant sedan design was strange, the wagon was bizarre. If you didn't want to be stared at, you didn't want to drive a Valiant wagon. Valiants were trimmed more like full-size cars with the up level V-200 at a point somewhere between the Bel Air and Impala.

Remember the Rambler American? The little two-door sedans and two-door wagons had sold well in 1959 and a new four-door sedan was cobbled up to fit the 100-inch wheelbase for 1960. Unlike the little two-doors, which were fairly appealing, this four-door was oddly proportioned. The 195.6-cid L-head six-cylinder developed 90 horses at 3,800 rpm (torque: 150 lbs.-ft. at 1,600 rpm). Americans were available with manual overdrive transmissions. Compared to the Corvair, the American was 1.7 inches shorter in overall length, 5.9 inches taller and 6.1 inches wider. The technology was certainly dated but the American had a good reputation, a low price and performed its duties.

VW, the odd little throwback to 1930s Germany, continued to win over Americans. The VW, which built a reputation on changing only things that needed to be changed, made a few changes for 1960. Big stuff like a deep-dish steering wheel, vinyl headlining, redesigned seats, new outside door handles and redesigned sun visors. Available as a two-door, two-door with sunroof

MADLER
8-1-58

19920

This full-scale drawing was photographed on August 1, 1958. While carrying Impala identification, the single quarter panel molding and lack of front fender ornamentation suggest that this is really a Bel Air. The wheel covers have simulated lug nuts and dust covers.

and convertible on a 94.5-inch wheelbase, the little four-passenger beetle was powered by a 73 cid horizontally opposed four-cylinder air-cooled engine which produced 36 horsepower at 3,700 rpm.

While much of the publicity surrounding the 1960 model year related to compact cars, the volume was still in low-priced full-sized cars. That was traditionally Chevrolet territory. 1960 was a very competitive year with a number of fresh, new designs aimed right at Chevrolet. Chevrolet, with a radical new design in 1959, was fielding a facelift for 1960. Over the past few years, Chevrolet and Ford had been alternating back and forth with designs that were either too conservative for the public or too radical. 1960 was Chevrolet's year to retrench after the very dramatic designs of 1959. Ford was coming off a year in which the rather conservative styling had played well with the public.

This time it was Ford's turn to get a little ahead of the public. Utilizing an all-new chassis, Ford's 119-inch wheelbase was identical to that of Chevrolet, but at 213.7 inches overall, the Ford was longer by 2.9 inches. Just 10 years earlier, in 1950, the Cadillac Series 61 was two inches shorter than this Ford. Standing 55 inches tall the Ford was an inch lower than the Chevrolet. It was also about 100 pounds heavier. The styling, while a radical departure from previous models, was clean. The wraparound windshield was gone and so was most of the body-side sculpturing. The theme now incorporated long straight lines. The unusually wide hood sloped downward to give the driver a good view of the road. A single bright molding rose from the front bumper to frame the edge of the fender, following the belt line the entire length of the body, finally curving around the corner of the horizontal fin to terminate at the decklid cut line.

Viewed from the front, the grille opening was wall-to-wall with the dual headlamp units at each end. The rear view revealed a departure from the previous round tail lamps. The Starliner two-door hardtop with its near-fastback profile was a dramatic break from the very angular 1959 side view. Sedan rooflines were closer to those of 1959 but most featured a large, curved backlight (rear windshield), the exception being the Galaxie four-door hardtop which continued the tunneled, near flat backlight.

The 1960 full-size Fords were available in three trim levels: Fairlane, Fairlane 500 and top-of-the-line Galaxie. These series were aimed directly at the Biscayne, Bel Air and Impala. Station wagons were treated as a separate series. The wagons were styled to the point where practicality was sacrificed. While Chevrolet elected to use a squared-off rear end to maximize cargo length at the belt and roof, Ford went with an extreme forward slope at the tailgate resulting in a greatly reduced cargo length at the roof. Ford also chose to retain the two-piece tailgate with a huge window in the liftgate portion.

Plymouth, which had been struggling with a well-deserved reputation for quality control problems, made serious changes for 1960. Like all full size Chrysler products (except Imperial) for 1960, Plymouth went

This 1960 Corvair 500 four-door sedan prototype was attached to a 5th wheel testing device in September 1959. The pronounced, overhanging character line ran completely around the body.

unitized (Unibody) construction. In this design a separate front stub frame carried the engine, front suspension and front sheet metal. The old Flathead 6 was finally retired having been replaced by a modern 225-cid OHV "Slant 6" which was rated at 145 horses at 4,000 rpm. By 1960 tall fins had pretty much had their day and fins were either disappearing or getting smaller. Except at Chrysler, which had scored a home run with fins in 1957 and thought there was still some life there. Plymouth tested this theory in 1960 and paid dearly. Of course, it wasn't just the fins. The Plymouth grille was flat and deeply tunneled beneath a rolled under hood, which gave Plymouth's face the look of a toothless old man. The front fenders had an odd character line and even the interior featured a strange floating instrument cluster. If all this were not bad enough, Dodge, which had always been priced above Plymouth, was given the Dart at very close to the price of a Plymouth. The Dart (not to be confused with the compact car introduced in 1963) was a well-styled Plymouth-derived product that sucked up Plymouth buyers like a sponge, attracting plenty of Ford and Chevrolet conquest sales along the way. When the year was over, Dodge was sitting on over 30,000 unbuilt orders. Nearly all of those would-be buyers drifted away in 1961 when they did the ugly thing to Dodge – but that's another story.

American Motors, which had been fielding several lines of vehicles, had a winner in the standard size Rambler Six or Rambler V-8. An extensive facelift gave the 1960 models a fresh look. The wraparound windshield was eliminated and the backlight enlarged for improved glass area. The tail fins were chopped off and a gentle line rose at the leading edge of the front door to form a small horizontal fin that swept across the decklid. The sensible but clean and contemporary Rambler was sized about mid-way between the Corvair and the Impala. This was just exactly the right size for that growing number of buyers who felt deserted by the Big Three.

1960 had been an exciting year for the auto industry. In the battle of the compacts, the Falcon (435,676) handily out-produced the Corvair (250,007) while the Valiant (194,292) managed a distant third. The Rambler American (120,603) was probably more competitive than its maker ever anticipated. VW (159,995) was slotted between the Valiant and the American. While it is certain that Chevrolet had hoped for much better results in Corvair's first year, the stellar performance of the regular size Chevrolet (1,391,485) against the new regular size Ford (911,034) must have been very satisfying. It should be recognized that the profit margin is usually much greater on regular size cars. So, while Ford sold a lot of lower profit Falcons, Chevrolet sold a big lot of high profit big Chevys.

Another bit of happy news for Chevrolet was that, in regular size wagons, it beat the "wagon master," Ford, by almost 41,000 vehicles. Dodge's Dart (306,603) outsold Plymouth (253,430). The product decisions that Chrysler made at that time undermined Plymouth's viability as that corporation's value leader and started the chain of events that would lead to the marque's death 40 years later.

The rear passenger compartment of a 1960 Impala convertible is dominated by the two-tone pattern vinyl (houndstooth) seating surfaces surrounded by two shades of leather-grain vinyl. The convertible floor covering was a combination of rayon carpet (on tunnel areas only) and vinyl coated rubber mat. Note the bright seat end caps.

This Bel Air two-door sedan shows the new two-tone paint treatment in which the tail plane area remains body color. At the rear, the cove area is painted body color on Bel Air trim level only. A major styling element was the canted fender windsplit, which led into the doors and ultimately formed the edges of the tail plane. The model 1619 V-8 had an advertised price of $2,545. The wheel covers added $22, two-tone paint $16, and whitewalls $31.

Model 1867, an Impala V-8 convertible, displays the new, simplified front-end treatment in which the full width grille incorporates an oval emblem in the center of a wide bar connecting the widely spaced dual headlight units. A bright molding surrounds the entire grille opening. The advertised price was $2,954. The whitewalls were extra at $31; the wheel covers cost $22.

This full-size fiberglass model sport sedan, photographed on October 24, 1958, shows a proposed concave grille. Bel Air rear door trim is used. The production front fender windsplit at headlight level, about where that "Chevrolet" script is located, is not shown on this vehicle.

The Impala instrument panel featured a wall-to-wall molding over the bright embossed facing. The armrest incorporated the door handle on a very colorful door panel featuring two shades of leather-grain vinyl and a large insert of two-tone cloth-pattern vinyl, some bright moldings and a dash of Mylar. The seating surfaces used nylon-faced two-tone pattern cloth with bolsters of leather-grain vinyl. The floor covering was deep-pile rayon carpeting.

A mid-year entry was this attractive model 10527 1960 Corvair 500 Club Coupe. Wheel trim rings, whitewalls and bumper guards add to the appearance of this low-line coupe. The weight of this 180-inch-long vehicle was just 2,270 pounds.

**This six-passenger, two-door Brookwood wagon is a six-cylinder (no V on the tailgate) model 1115. It had an overall length of 210.8 inches on a 119-inch wheelbase with overall height of 56.3 inches.**

After a rest of several years, the mid-level two-door hardtop returned to Chevrolet in the form of this very clean Bel Air Sport Coupe. This model, with an advertised price of $2,596 (V-8 model) was just $108 less than a similar Impala sport coupe, which undoubtedly accounts for its scarcity today.

The Corvair 700 four-door sedan was, at introduction, the top of the line. The bright moldings outlining the windshield, the roof rain rail and encircling the car at the character line were 700 series features. A close look reveals that those wheel trim rings have a series of Chevrolet "Bow-Ties."

Seen in a light color, the Biscayne four-door sedan, model 1119 (6) or 1219 (V-8), was less grim than the more common dark colors. If you think the rear overhang is rather extreme, you're right. It measures 59.2 inches. That's half the wheelbase. Surprisingly, the turning diameter of 43.6 feet was smaller than that of Ford or Plymouth in 1960.

Why would anyone want to set up a fancy glamour shot of a 1960 Impala and not use the optional (at $22!) wheel covers? This angle shows the new ribbed anodized aluminum front license plate carrier and the turn signal lights in the valance panel.

This is one of the test mules that was constructed to evaluate the suspension and powertrain of the new Corvairs. The Michigan Manufacturer's license plate is dated 1958. Test mules continue to be used frequently to test secret components on public roads.

The 1960 Bel Air Sport Sedan was just the ticket for the traditional, more conservative Chevrolet buyer who couldn't relate to the 1959, or even, 1960 Impalas. The reflections on the hood accentuate the twin hood windsplits. The rear antenna was a $7.95 option or it could be included in radio packages for dealer installation.

An inspector is making notes as this model 1135 Brookwood six-cylinder, four-door, six-passenger wagon prepares to enter a waiting world on September 28, 1959.

The Impala four-door sedan looked good in black (and most other colors) but this one needs the $22 wheel covers. The contrasting color insert on the rear door and quarter panel was standard on Impalas. An Impala and Bel Air characteristic was the wide molding recessed into the door and the rear quarter panel character line.

There were no exterior differences distinguishing this 1960 Corvette from its 1959 predecessor. The "Fuel Injection" script warns the drivers of lesser vehicles not to embarrass themselves at the traffic light. The 2,840-pound vehicle had an advertised price of $3,872.

Located on Detroit's northwest side at the corner of Seven-Mile Road and Strathmoor, Hanley Dawson was a good size operation in 1960. A Corvair 500 four-door shares the floor with a pair of regular Chevrolets.

The least expensive regular size six-passenger Chevrolet was this model 1111 six-cylinder Biscayne two-door sedan with an advertised price of $2,262. A close look will reveal that the bright molding in the recessed portion of the body character line is thinner than that used on Impala and Bel Air models.

This is the interior of a 1960 Corvette with removable hardtop, four-speed manual transmission and power windows. The handy parcel box, introduced in 1959, can be seen under the passenger assist bar.

This Bel Air interior shows the two-tone leather-grain vinyl door panel and the nylon-faced tri-tone pattern cloth-seating surfaces. The full width instrument panel molding was carried over from 1959. Deep pile rayon carpet covered the tunnel areas and colored vinyl coated rubber mat was used in the foot wells and for flat surfaces.

The Corvair's rear-mounted engine was air-cooled. Do you suppose that had something to do with the camel on a rope? The vehicle is a model 700 four-door sedan as evidenced by the bright moldings on the character line, roof rain rail and surrounding the rear window.

The 1960 Impala had a nicely styled convertible top. While some convertibles lose much of their grace when the top goes up, this one still had a sporty look. That look was further enhanced by the twin rear antennas. The left antenna was a dummy; the right was functional. The pair added $14.70 to the cost. The wheel covers were $22; the whitewalls were $31.

Remember that earlier studio shot with the gates of the Greenbriar? Here's how it was done. The vehicle is a 1960 Nomad six-passenger, four-door station wagon. The Nomad was the fanciest of Chevrolet's line of regular-size wagons. In a rear view, the Nomad was readily identified by the vertically textured bright cove applique.

Fuel injection was no longer available with regular-size Chevrolets for 1960. This Ramjet 283 was still available for Corvette in 250-hp and 290-hp versions with four-speed manual transmission only. This is the 250-hp fuelie, which listed for $484; the 290-hp motor cost the same, $484.

A new 1960 Impala V-8 Sport Coupe, model 1637, is going for its first ride. This car had an advertised price of $2,704 and weighed 3,530 pounds. It stood just 54 inches tall and like all other regular 1960 Chevrolets, had a 119-inch wheelbase.

The crest in the grille emblem signifies that this Biscayne four-door sedan is a model 1119. The new upswept front bumper ends can be clearly seen. The ornament on the rear door is a Biscayne exclusive. Bel Air and Impala models used a similar but larger ornament.

The two-tone 1960 Corvair 700 four-door sedan is parked between a 1959 Impala Sport Sedan and a 1959 Nomad. The object was to show that a Corvair could be parked in spaces that drivers of large cars had to pass up. The overall length of this Corvair was 180.0 inches, about 2.5 feet shorter than that Impala.

Add a set of $22 wheel covers, whitewalls at $31 and $16 worth of two-tone paint to a mid-level Bel Air four-door sedan, model 1619 (V-8) or model 1519 (6), and you've got a pretty perky Chevy.

The 1958 XP700 Corvette show car was recycled in 1960. Among the 1960 updates was a see-through plastic top.

In profile the Corvair 500 Club Coupe looked like a larger car than its actual overall length of 180.0 inches. Rear overhang of 41.7 inches was less than that of either the Falcon or Valiant.

The film crew pauses for a moment of levity on the set at GM Photographic's Royal Oak, Michigan studio. It certainly makes a statement about the spacious luggage compartment of the 1960 Impala Convertible.

The rear seat occupant of this 1960 Corvair 700 four-door sedan has adequate space for a short trip but not much "wiggle room" for a long one. Notice the plain door panel insert.

The gentlemen are about to load a quantity of rice into the cargo area of this 1960 Brookwood two-door, six-passenger station wagon. With a cargo floor length of 94.4 inches and a width of 46.0 inches between the wheelhouses, and a floor to ceiling height of 32.1 inches, they could load a lot more rice than the tires could support.

This full size clay model photographed on March 12, 1958 shows that the stylists once considered running the recessed area the full length of the character line and extending the mid-body crease all the way up to the front wheel opening.

The 1960 Bel Air Sport Coupe looks lower than its 54.0-inch height. The only front fender ornamentation was the "Bel Air" script with integral crest. The license plate frame, whitewalls, and wheel covers were extra cost items.

The Biscayne Utility two-door sedan was the lowest-priced regular-size Chevrolet. The model 1121 (6), a 3,480-pound car had a delivered price of $2,160. The whitewalls added another $31.

The 1960 Corvette shown here is a fuel injected car with a removable fiberglass hardtop, whitewalls and a painted cove area. This was the only 1960 Chevrolet with standard full wheel covers.

Now in its second year, the El Camino was one sleek hauler. The grille emblem, consisting of a crest and a V, indicates the presence of a 283 engine. While the trim level is that of a Biscayne, the quarter panel "missile" is from the Bel Air level.

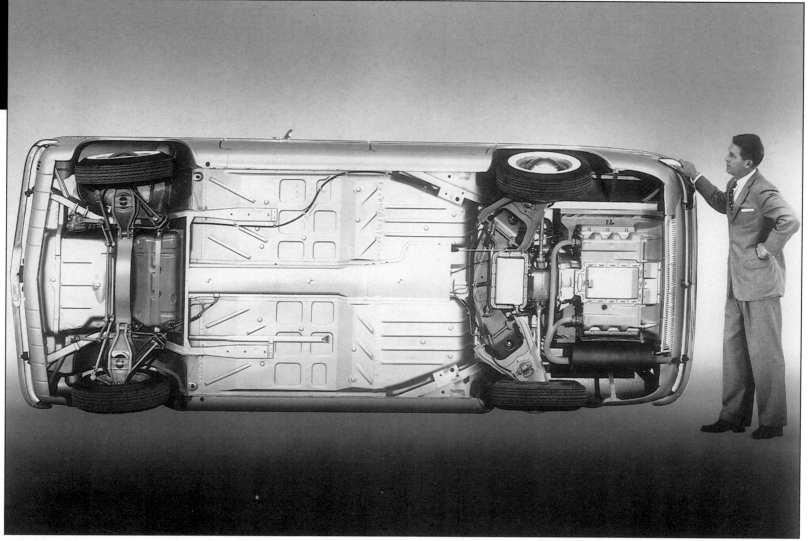

This 1960 Corvair has been rotated on its side to show the very clean underbody detail. At the rear, the horizontally opposed six-cylinder OHV engine is behind the transaxle (this one has Powerglide, note the pan). The gas tank is the dark object behind the front axle.

The full plastic rear window can be seen on this Impala convertible. The 3,635-pound car rode on 8:00 x 14 tires. The position of the shift lever tells us that this car has an automatic transmission in the "park" position.

The 1960 Corvette had a fairly spacious trunk with a ribbed rubber mat. In 1963 the trunk would be eliminated.

This shot shows the sequence involved in folding the rear seat of a Corvair 700 four-door sedan. The folding seat option was available for 500 or 700 series Corvairs and gave a 17-cubic-foot load space.

**Shown under the glove box door on a 1960 Impala convertible is the accessory litter container. No flimsy little bag, this container was removable and made of expandable waterproof plastic. The litter container was available for just $4.50.**

The Powerglide selector for the 1960 Corvair was conveniently located below the instrument cluster with a lighted window just to the right of the ignition switch. This location was quite secure in that children would be unlikely to kick the lever while the vehicle was in motion.

The Parkwood was the six-passenger, four-door wagon sharing the Bel Air trim level. The V on the tailgate verifies that this is a model 1635, a V-8 model. The 3,950-pound wagon had an advertised price of $2,854. The wheel covers were priced at $22, the 8:00 x 14 whitewalls, $35.

At announcement time, the 1960 Corvair 700 was a little plain outside, very plain inside. The mid-year introduction of the Monza resolved that. The moldings that encircled the car at the character line were deleted, a rocker panel spear was added, as were chrome vents beneath the back window. Monza emblems were placed on the front fenders; slender whitewalls and sporty wheel covers completed the package.

This 1960 Biscayne Utility two-door sedan was actually a three-passenger car. The rear seat area was modified to carry cargo and luggage. It was a good choice for businessmen who wanted a vehicle that hauled like a small truck but looked and acted like a car.

This 1960 Corvette has the convertible top and one of the Ramjet Fuel Injection 283-cid engines developing either 250 hp or 290 hp.

The mid-year 1960 Corvair Monza Club Coupe had a very impressive and sporty vinyl interior with a deluxe steering wheel with horn ring, bucket seats, full carpet with heel pad, specific door trim and instrument panel trim. This very effectively addressed the most serious criticism of the Corvair's appearance.

This 1960 Corvette with convertible top, fuel injection and aftermarket driving lights competed in a 1961 rally at the continental divide on a snowy day.

**Remember the Corvair test mule? This is the driver's compartment. It was a gauge lover's delight. At least 15 gauges were added.**

At the right edge of this shot we can see the bright end caps on the Corvair Monza's bucket seats. Also visible are chrome seat back ashtrays. At this angle the seat cushion appears to be pretty close to the floor.

'60

This is just kind of a neat shot. A little soft perhaps, and the car, a 1960 Bel Air four-door sedan doesn't even have wheel covers, but it does have two-tone paint and whitewalls. Whatever, the horse, the girl and the landscape are all neat.

The mid-year Corvair Monza is shown here. The window reveal moldings and sporty wheel covers add to the luxury look. At $2,238, just $189 above the 700 Club Coupe, the Monza quickly helped to establish the Corvair's sporty image.

**This photo from January 2, 1958 shows a 1960 Chevrolet Sport Coupe that has Buick overtones in the front, Oldsmobile in the rear.**

This is a lineup of three 1960 Corvair 500 four-door sedans with Illinois dealer license plates. Americans were accustomed to big chrome grilles. Many felt that the concave Corvair front end was too plain. Within a few months of the Corvair's introduction, some entrepreneur began selling an eggcrate grille that could be attached to the front of a Corvair. It wasn't a big seller.

This 1960 Biscayne front passenger compartment shows the seating surfaces of nylon-faced pattern cloth and the leather-grain vinyl door panels. The floor covering is a colored vinyl-coated rubber mat. This vehicle has a manual transmission.

**What an odd combination. This 1960 Impala Sport Coupe is wearing two-tone paint, base hubcaps, blackwall tires and dual rear antennas.**

**The grille emblem, a gold V over crossed flags, signifies a 348 V-8 engine. A silver V over a Chevrolet crest is found on 283 V-8 vehicles. A crest with no V is worn by six-cylinder vehicles.**

This is a line of Corvair Turbo-Air six-cylinder engines. The horizontally opposed air-cooled engine relied on the belt driven fan seen below the central air cleaner. This belt also drove the generator. When a Corvair threw the belt, cooling was lost instantly. Most owners carried a spare belt and the special wrench required for the repair.

This four-car carrier was used for local deliveries. A 1960 Impala Sport Sedan rides over the cab. An Impala Sport Coupe is stacked over a Bel Air four-door sedan and a Bel Air two-door sedan.

In 1961 Chevrolet trooped a small auto show, "The Chevy Aerosphere Show," to shopping center parking lots. The concept was field tested in 1960, as shown here. A 1960 Brookwood two-door, six-passenger wagon and a 1960 Corvette were part of the outside display. The lady in the background seems surprised to find that this thing has sprung up overnight at her local A&P.

Here's another view of that Aerosphere, which was supported by air pressure. The whole display could be knocked down and moved to the next city with very little fuss. A 1960 Nomad is displayed at the right.

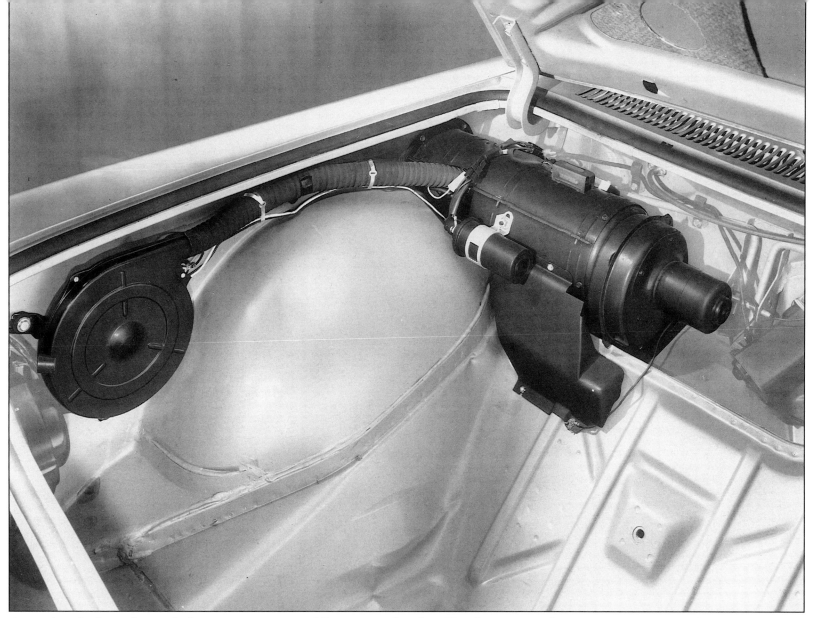

Corvairs, being air-cooled cars, were not able to use the familiar hot water heater. A rather ineffective heater drew hot air from the engine and forced it into the passenger compartment. This is the accessory gasoline heater and defroster located in the front luggage compartment. The dealer's cost on this unit was $53.95. Retail installed prices were around $100.

**This 1960 Falcon is close to a base model with a radio and whitewalls.**

Ford's all-new Galaxie Starliner two-door hardtop was directly competitive with the Impala Sport Coupe. The Ford's drooping nose had some detractors. Overall length was 213.7 inches, almost 3 inches longer than Impala.

'60

A 1960 Ford Fairlane 500 and a 1960 Bel Air are shown here. They both featured mid-level trim. The Ford used a very large, curved backlight (rear window).

**The pushbutton door handles were new on the VW for 1960. Unseen were the new vinyl headliner and anti-sway bar.**

The rear door, quarter panel and windshield were nicely restyled on this standard size 1960 Rambler. This one is a pretty rare car because it is a Rebel V-8, a four-door hardtop, and it has factory air conditioning, (the bright oval on the front door signifies air conditioning). Some buyers preferred the Rambler's 189.5 inch overall length to the Impala's 210.8 inches, especially for city driving.

The Belvedere was the mid-level trim for Plymouth in 1960. This two-door hardtop was a Bel Air competitor. The grille, front fender and "jump up" fin styling left a lot of buyers cold.

The Dart series of Dodges was priced nose-to-nose with Chevrolet, Ford and Plymouth. This is a Phoenix, the best Dart. The public loved it, hated the Plymouth. More than a few Chevrolet intenders were reeled in as well.

MADLER
1-21-60

26848

Shown in the styling dome at the GM Technical Center are a mid-level Ford Fairlane and a low-line Plymouth Savoy. The Plymouth front end seems to be way above recommended ride height, a condition that could be corrected by adjusting the torsion bars.

The 1960 Valiant V-200 was the top-of-the-line. It was one of those love-it-or-hate-it cars. Its wheelbase was 1.5 inches shorter than the Corvair's but it was 3.7 inches longer overall.

**Studebaker's crisp little Lark convertible was a compact-size alternative to the full-size cars. The Roman numerals on the fender identify this as a V-8.**

# 1960 CHEVROLET MODEL CHART

| TYPE | IMPALA | | BEL AIR | | BISCAYNE | | BISCAYNE FLEETMASTER | | WAGONS | |
|---|---|---|---|---|---|---|---|---|---|---|
| | 6 CYL. | 8 CYL. | 6 CYL. | 8 CYL. | 6 CYL. | 8 CYL. | 6 CYL. | 8 CYL. | 6 CYL. | 8 CYL. |
| 2-Door Sedan | | | 1511 | 1611 | 1111 | 1211 | | | | |
| 2-Door Utility Sedan | | | | | 1121 | 1221 | | | | |
| 4-Door Sedan | 1719 | 1819 | 1519 | 1619 | 1169 | 1269 | 1369 | 1469 | | |
| Sport Coupe  (2-dr. hdtp.) | 1737 | 1837 | 1537 | 1637 | | | | | | |
| Sport Sedan (4-dr. hdtp.) | 1739 | 1839 | 1539 | 1639 | | | | | | |
| Convertible | 1767 | 1867 | | | | | | | | |
| Brookwood 2-Door 6-pass. | | | | | | | | | 1115 | 1215 |
| Brookwood 4-Door 6-pass. | | | | | | | | | 1135 | 1235 |
| Parkwood 4-Door 6-pass. | | | | | | | | | 1535 | 1635 |
| Kingswood 4-Door 9-pass. | | | | | | | | | 1545 | 1645 |
| Nomad 4-Door 6-pass. | | | | | | | | | 1735 | 1835 |

# 1960 CHEVROLET CORVAIR MODEL CHART

| TYPE | 500 | 700 DELUXE | 900 MONZA |
|---|---|---|---|
| 2-Door Club Coupe | 0527 | 0727 | 0927 |
| 4-Door Sedan | 0569 | 0769 | |

# 1960 FOUR-DOOR SEDAN COMPARISONS

| | CHEVROLET BISCAYNE | FORD CUSTOM | PLYMOUTH SAVOY | RAMBLER 6 | STUDEBAKER LARK | RAMBLER AMERICAN | CHEVROLET CORVAIR | FORD FALCON | PLYMOUTH VALIANT |
|---|---|---|---|---|---|---|---|---|---|
| Wheelbase | 119.0" | 119.0" | 118.0" | 108.0" | 108.5" | 100.0" | 108.0" | 109.5" | 106.5" |
| Overall Length | 210.8" | 213.7" | 209.4" | 189.5" | 175.0" | 178.3" | 180.0" | 181.2" | 183.7" |
| Front Overhang | 32.6" | 33.9" | 33.2" | 32.1" | 26.43" | — | 30.3" | 29.4" | 29.2" |
| Rear Overhang | 59.2" | 60.7" | 58.2" | 49.4" | 40.06" | — | 41.7" | 42.3" | 48.0" |
| Height (design load) | 56.0" | 55.0" | 54.8" | 57.3" | 57.5" | 57.2" | 51.3" | 54.5" | 53.3" |
| Width | 80.8" | 81.5" | 78.6" | 72.2" | 71.375" | 73.0" | 66.9" | 70.3" | 70.4" |
| Tread-front | 60.3" | 61.0" | 60.9" | 57.75" | 57.37" | 54.62" | 54.0" | 55.0" | 56.0" |
| Tread-rear | 59.3" | 60.0" | 59.6" | 58.0" | 56.5" | 55.0" | 54.0" | 54.5" | 55.5" |
| Weight (curb) | 3,715 lbs. | 3,812 lbs. | 3,550 lbs. | 3,038 lbs. | 2,728 lbs. | 2,614 lbs. | 2,375 lbs. | 2,424 lbs. | 2,725 lbs. |
| Turning Diameter | 43.6 ft. | 45.95 ft. | 45.3 ft. | 39.3 ft. | 40.0 ft. | 37.9 ft. | 41.6 ft. | 40.8 ft. | 39.6 ft. |
| Front Headroom | 36.1" | 33.5" | 33.3" | 35.0" | 36.0" | 35.25" | 33.6" | 33.8" | 33.6" |
| Rear Headroom | 34.3" | 33.9" | 33.5" | 34.0" | 35.0" | 34.0" | 32.4" | 32.7" | 33.4" |
| Front Legroom | 45.5" | 43.3" | 45.3" | 43.0" | 44.0" | 44.0" | 43.8" | 43.3" | 43.0" |
| Rear Legroom | 42.5" | 41.6" | 42.1" | 40.0" | 39.0" | 37.5" | 31.5" | 39.4" | 39.7" |
| Front Shoulder Room | 60.5" | 59.5" | 60.4" | 57.7" | 55.5" | 51.5" | 54.0" | 55.2" | 54.0" |
| Rear Shoulder Room | 59.0" | 61.1" | 59.8" | 57.6" | 54.5" | 49.75" | 51.9" | 54.8" | 54.1" |
| Front Hip Room | 65.3" | 62.1" | 63.8" | 59.75" | 59.5" | 58.0" | 58.4" | 57.0" | 56.8" |
| Rear Hip Room | 65.4" | 63.6" | 62.9" | 60.10" | 59.0" | 45.25" | 57.0" | 56.6" | 56.9" |

# 1960 CHEVROLET ENGINE CHART

| ENGINE | HP @ RPM | TORQUE @ RPM |
|---|---|---|
| 235.5 c.i.d. Base 6 | 135 @ 4000 | |
| 283 c.i.d. 2-bbl. V-8 (economy) | 170 @ 4200 | 275 @ 2200 |
| 283 c.i.d. 4-bbl. V-8 | 230 @ 4800 | 300 @ 3000 |
| 348 c.i.d. 4-bbl. V-8 | 250 @ 4400 | 355 @ 2800 |
| 348 c.i.d. 4-bbl. V-8* | 320 @ 5600 | 362 @ 3600 |
| 348 c.i.d. 3x2-bbl. V-8 | 280 @ 4800 | 355 @ 3200 |
| 348 c.i.d. 3x2-bbl. V-8* | 335 @ 5800 | 364 @ 3600 |
| 348 c.i.d. 4-bbl. V-8* | 305 @ 5200 | 355 @ 3400 |

* Special Camshaft

# 1960 CHEVROLET CORVETTE ENGINE CHART

| ENGINE | HP @ RPM | TORQUE @ RPM |
|---|---|---|
| 283 c.i.d. 4-bbl. V-8 | 230 @ 4800 | 300 @ 3000 |
| 283 c.i.d. 2x4-bbl. V-8 | 245 @ 5000 | 300 @ 3800 |
| 283 c.i.d. 2x4-bbl. V-8* | 270 @ 6000 | 285 @ 4200 |
| 283 c.i.d. Fuel Injection V-8 | 250 @ 5200 | 305 @ 4400 |
| 283 c.i.d. Fuel Injection V-8* | 290 @ 6200 | 295 @ 5100 |

* Special Camshaft

# 1960 CORVAIR ENGINE CHART

| ENGINE | HP @ RPM | TORQUE @ RPM |
|---|---|---|
| 140 c.i.d. 1-2-bbl. 6 | 80 @ 4400 | 125 @ 2400 |

Horizontally opposed OHV air cooled

# 1960 FORD ENGINE CHART

| ENGINE | HP @ RPM | TORQUE @ RPM |
|---|---|---|
| 223 c.i.d. 1-bbl. 6 | 145 @ 4000 | 206 @ 2000 |
| 292 c.i.d. 2-bbl. V-8 | 185 @ 4200 | 292 @ 2200 |
| 352 c.i.d. 2-bbl. V-8 | 235 @ 4400 | 350 @ 2400 |
| 352 c.i.d. 4-bbl. V-8 | 300 @ 4600 | 381 @ 2800 |
| 352 c.i.d. 4-bbl. V-8 | 360 @ 6000 | 380 @ 3400 |

# 1960 FORD FALCON ENGINE CHART

| ENGINE | HP @ RPM | TORQUE @ RPM |
|---|---|---|
| 144.3 c.i.d. 1-bbl. 6 | 90 @ 4200 | 138 @ 2000 |

## 1960 RAMBLER ENGINE CHART

| ENGINE | HP @ RPM | TORQUE @ RPM |
|---|---|---|
| 195.6 c.i.d. 1-bbl. 6 | 127 @ 4200 | 180 @ 1600 |
| 195.6 c.i.d. 2-bbl. 6 | 138 @ 4500 | 185 @ 1800 |
| 250 c.i.d. 2-bbl. V-8 | 200 @ 4900 | 245 @ 2500 |
| 250 c.i.d. 4-bbl. V-8 | 215 @ 4900 | 260 @ 2500 |

## 1960 RAMBLER AMERICAN ENGINE CHART

| ENGINE | HP @ RPM | TORQUE @ RPM |
|---|---|---|
| 195.6 c.i.d. L-head 6 | 90 @ 3800 | 150 @ 1600 |
| 195.6 c.i.d. 1-bbl. OHV 6 | 125 @ 4200 | 180 @ 1600 |

## 1960 STUDEBAKER LARK ENGINE CHART

| ENGINE | HP @ RPM | TORQUE @ RPM |
|---|---|---|
| 169.6 c.i.d. 1-bbl. 6 (L-head) | 90 @ 4000 | 145 @ 2000 |
| 259.2 c.i.d. 2-bbl. V-8 | 180 @ 4500 | 260 @ 2800 |
| 259.2 c.i.d. 4-bbl. V-8 | 195 @ 4500 | 265 @ 3000 |

## 1960 PLYMOUTH ENGINE CHART

| ENGINE | HP @ RPM | TORQUE @ RPM |
|---|---|---|
| 225 c.i.d. 1-bbl. 6 | 145 @ 4000 | 215 @ 2800 |
| 318 c.i.d. 2-bbl. V-8 | 230 @ 4400 | 340 @ 2400 |
| 318 c.i.d. 4-bbl. V-8 | 260 @ 4400 | 345 @ 2800 |
| 361 c.i.d. 4-bbl. V-8 | 305 @ 4800 | 395 @ 3500 |
| 361 c.i.d. 2-bbl. V-8 | 310 @ 4800 | 435 @ 2800 |

## 1960 VALIANT ENGINE CHART

| ENGINE | HP @ RPM | TORQUE @ RPM |
|---|---|---|
| 170 c.i.d. 1-bbl. 6 | 101 @ 4400 | 155 @ 2400 |
| 170 c.i.d. Hyper Pak 6 | 148 @ 5200 | 153 @ 4200 |

## 1960 CHEVROLET
## COLOR CHART

- Tuxedo Black*
- Ermine White*
- Sateen Silver*
- Shadow Gray
- Tasco Turquoise*
- Cascade Green*
- Jade Green*
- Fawn Beige
- Horizon Blue*
- Royal Blue*
- Roman Red*
- Suntan Copper
- Crocus Cream
- Ermine White/Tuxedo Black*
- Ermine White/Sateen Silver*
- Ermine White/Tasco Turquoise*
- Ermine White/Roman Red
- Jade Green/Cascade Green*
- Cascade Green/Jade Green*
- Royal Blue/Horizon Blue*
- Fawn Beige/Suntan Copper
- Horizon Blue/Royal Blue*
- Sateen Silver/Shadow Gray
- Ermine White/Cascade Green
- Ermine White/Horizon Blue
* Also available on Corvair

## 1960 CHEVROLET
## CORVETTE
## COLOR CHART

### SOLID COLORS

- Tuxedo Black
- Horizon Blue
- Sateen Silver
- Ermine White
- Honduras Maroon
- Cascade Green
- Roman Red
- Tasco Turquoise

### TWO-TONE COLORS

- Tuxedo Black/Sateen Silver
- Ermine White/Sateen Silver
- Horizon Blue/Ermine White
- Roman Red/Ermine White
- Sateen Silver/Ermine White
- Honduras Maroon/Ermine White
- Tasco Turquoise/Ermine White
- Cascade Green/Ermine White